SARAH MOORE AND ALEX NEWBURY

LEGAL AID IN CRISIS

Assessing the impact of reform

POLICY PRESS SHORTS POLICY & PRACTICE

First published in Great Britain in 2017 by

Policy Press
University of Bristol
1-9 Old Park Hill
Bristol
BS2 8BB
UK
+44 (0)117 954 5940
pp-info@bristol.ac.uk
www.policypress.co.uk

North America office:
Policy Press
c/o The University of Chicago Press
1427 East 60th Street
Chicago, IL 60637, USA
t: +1 773 702 7700
f: +1 773 702 9756
sales@press.uchicago.edu
www.press.uchicago.edu

© Policy Press 2017

British Library Cataloguing in Publication Data
A catalogue record for this book is available from the British Library.

Library of Congress Cataloging-in-Publication Data
A catalog record for this book has been requested.

ISBN 978-1-4473-3545-0 (paperback)
ISBN 978-1-4473-3547-4 (ePub)
ISBN 978-1-4473-3548-1 (Mobi)
ISBN 978-1-4473-3546-7 (ePdf)

Cover design by Policy Press
Front cover: image kindly supplied by www.alamy.com
Printed and bound in Great Britain by CMP, Poole
Policy Press uses environmentally responsible print partners

For all those who get lost in the process

Contents

List of abbreviations

CAB	Citizens Advice Bureau
CSJPS	Civil and Social Justice Panel Survey
ECF	Exceptional case funding
LAB	Legal Aid Board
LASPO	Legal Aid, Sentencing and Punishment of Offenders Act 2012
LiP	Litigant in person
LSC	Legal Services Commission

Acknowledgements

Our thanks go to our colleagues in the Department of Social and Policy Sciences at Bath University and Brighton Business School at the University of Brighton. This project has been some time in the making, and we're lucky enough to work at universities that have given us the necessary thinking space to work through our ideas. We'd also like to thank our colleagues at CLOCK whose commitment to access to justice has been a huge source of inspiration for us. We are grateful also for Hector Murphy's assistance with sourcing information and to Jo Wilding for giving valuable and thoughtful input on the finished draft of the manuscript.

We've been supported throughout the writing of this book by an excellent editorial team who immediately 'got' the project and its importance. We'd like to thanks Victoria Pittman and Rebecca Tomlinson for all their help and input.

We would particularly like to thank our partners, Alex and Paul, for their support during the writing of this book: for endless cups of tea; and for fielding the lion's share of school runs and nursery pick-ups. We would also like to thank Sylvie, Fraser and Tom for showing us on a daily basis that family matters. And now on to other family matters.

1
LEGAL AID IN CRISIS

Introduced in England and Wales as part of the mid-20th-century move towards welfarism, legal aid is currently undergoing the most radical set of reforms in its 65-year history. This is part of a global shift. Many economically developed countries have embarked on sweeping reforms to legal aid, and this book considers the cuts in England and Wales in this context. Given the scale and nature of the shift in legal aid provision, the issue has received surprisingly little media attention. As we write this introductory chapter, most national newspapers are running a story about the publication of a United Nation's report on the effect of United Kingdom (UK) austerity politics on human rights (Committee on Economic, Social and Cultural Rights, 2016). Though the report is excoriating about legal aid reform, identifying it as a particular source of concern, none of the news items even mention it. This is no accidental omission. Legal aid is routinely left out of news coverage of the social costs of austerity. We consider the relative lack of public debate about legal aid reform later. For now, and by way of introduction, we want to sketch out why we think legal aid reform matters and, more than that, why it should be seen as among the most important and impactful changes wrought by austerity politics.

Why does legal aid reform matter?

There are various problems we could latch on by way of introduction. Take the fact that the reforms have removed publicly funded legal support for most people seeking to challenge the state's decision on their social welfare arrangements. These cuts have recently come under scrutiny from the Low Commission (2014; 2015), a group formed to examine the impact of the legal aid reforms on social welfare law. The Commission's reports offer up meaningful suggestions for reform. Even so, they make for depressing reading. The abiding impression is that the cuts to legal aid have had perverse consequences, most notably that people seeking legal advice on most social welfare issues are now without publicly funded support unless they reach a crisis point. The removal of this safety net of support means that more people get to the point of teetering on the edge. Aside from any moral objections that might be raised to this arrangement, there is a profound lack of efficiency here. As the Low Commission (2014: vii) observes, the savings created by the cuts are likely to be eaten up by increased costs elsewhere in the system – to healthcare, local services and social services in particular.

An escalation in costs seems even more likely when we consider the wider economic and political context, and more specifically the deep cuts that have been made in the second decade of the twenty-first century to disability, employment, and housing benefits. Put in this context, legal aid reform is more than a simple matter of retrenchment. If the state has latterly reduced financial support for the most vulnerable in our society, the decision to limit people's access to judicial review of these life-changing decisions seems designed to entrench the resulting social inequalities. Add to this that the recent reforms have involved the Lord Chancellor having greater oversight of legal aid provision, and the argument that legal aid has become an instrument of the state becomes all the more persuasive.

There's a broader point to be made here: to remove funding for those challenging social welfare decisions means reducing citizens' ability to hold the state to account. It limits what the political philosopher Robert Forst (2014) calls our right to justification. The erosion of this basic yet fundamental right risks producing a sense that the state is like a runaway train, unimpeachable and unstoppable. This leap – from legal aid cuts to state-citizen relations – might seem like a stretch, but our point here is a simple one. Legal aid has a purpose beyond facilitating individual disputes; among other things, it underwrites the social contract in liberal democracies and helps sustain order. This is something that the recent reforms have ignored, and, in turn, part of this book's critical focus.

There are of course other ways of starting the story about legal aid reform in England and Wales. We could, for example, alight on the fact that legal aid support has been removed for all but a handful of private family law cases. Most cases that reach the court stage of proceedings involve people going through deeply acrimonious splits where communication has entirely broken down and contact with children is a matter of contention. These are not as a rule feckless people, draining a public resource simply because it's there, as those who have recently argued for legal aid cuts have frequently implied. As any legal aid lawyer will tell you, they tend to be desperate people who have come to court because everything else has failed. They include victims of domestic violence trying to separate from their partner. Under the most recent reforms, unless a victim of abuse has evidence, publicly funded legal aid is not available for them to pursue a family law case. It's a rule that's prompted international opprobrium, notably from the United Nations (again), who have criticised the new legal aid arrangements on the basis that they substantially disadvantage those women who have not formally disclosed experiences of domestic violence (Committee on the Elimination of All Forms of Discrimination against Women, 2013: 4). Recent research suggests that, even since the government relaxed the rules concerning domestic violence evidence and legal aid eligibility, roughly a third of women in this situation do not have the mandatory evidence to receive publicly funded legal assistance (Rights of Women et al, 2014). These women must choose, then, between spending a huge sum of money on legal representation (which in the majority of cases is likely to be entirely beyond their reach), representing themselves in the courtroom, or giving up and acceding to the demands of an abusive ex-partner.

These snapshot impressions of the new legal aid arrangements are important in reminding us that at the heart of many legal disputes are people caught up in painful disagreements – and that the reforms to legal aid place people in impossible situations. One aim of this book is to bring these lives, disputes and impossible situations into critical focus. We argue, in turn, that this more holistic approach should be essential to any assessment of the costs and value of legal aid. Also crucial, we argue, is a perspective that establishes legal aid's role in social welfare arrangements and recognises that this support is as fundamental to the wellbeing of a society as adequate health services and social security. This is particularly the case given that late modern societies are increasingly juridified – that is, an ever greater range of experiences and relationships has become subject to legal regulation. For these reasons, we see legal aid as a social policy concern, in accordance with how it was historically envisioned. Refocusing the debate to return to this original vision is crucial if we are to gain an understanding of what is at stake with legal aid reform. We return to these ideas in due course. We turn now to give a brief overview of the recent reforms.

What's changed?

The recent reforms are based on the Legal Aid, Sentencing and Punishment of Offenders Act 2012 (LASPO), which came into effect in April 2013. As discussed in Chapter Two, the story about legal aid reform doesn't start and end with LASPO. Nonetheless, this legislation has had a direct effect on legal aid provision. One such impact is a cut in funding that brings the government's annual spending on legal aid down from the 2009/10 peak of £2.2 billion to £1.6 billion in 2015/16 (Ministry of Justice and Legal Aid Agency, 2016a). Reducing solicitors' and barristers' fees and reorganising the way legal aid is provided has made some of these savings. However, changing what's in scope for legal aid provision has made the greater savings. Under LASPO, a number of areas of law are no longer covered. These include family law cases that do not involve evidence of domestic violence, child abuse, or child abduction, as well as almost all cases involving social welfare, housing, medical negligence, immigration, debt, and employment.

Thus, the brunt of the reforms has been borne by the civil legal aid scheme, in part because it has not been protected from the rising bill for criminal legal aid. For this reason, this book focuses on civil legal aid, and particularly family advocacy. Chapter Three provides a detailed discussion of the impact of the recent reforms on this area of law. By way of introduction, we want simply to note that there has been a particularly steep decrease in funding for legal advice, which consists mainly of conversations with solicitors to identify relevant support services and talk through possible courses of action and outcomes. Government funding for this form of support has dropped to around one third of its pre-LASPO level (Ministry of Justice and Legal Aid Agency, 2016a). It's a staggeringly sharp decrease within a three-year period, one that even took the Legal Aid Agency by surprise. In the year following the introduction of LASPO, the Agency funded 326,004 *fewer* acts of legal help than they anticipated (House of Commons Justice Committee, 2015: s3.12). In seeking to understand why, the House of Commons Justice Committee (2015) point to a lack of public knowledge around the new rules on eligibility, a situation that the government is only starting to attend to now, four years post-LASPO.

The cumulative effect of all this is that many support services have dropped off the map. Take for example the Footprints Child Contact Centre, established 18 years ago in the north of England. The Centre provides a safe space for separated parents to meet their children, something that is particularly important where accusations of domestic violence mean unsupervised contact is not possible. Dependent on referrals from solicitors, the Centre has experienced a huge reduction in its workload post-LASPO and in July 2016 announced its imminent closure (Law Society Gazette, 2016). This is by no means an isolated example. Over a fifth of Law Centres – front-line, non-profit organisations providing a mix of social and legal advice – have closed since LASPO came into effect (Law Centres Network, 2016). The Citizen's Advice Bureau (CAB) has also been adversely affected, with an 18.5% fall in its income since 2010, much of it due to the cuts to legal aid funding (Low Commission, 2014: 7). These organisations constitute the infrastructure of legal support services in England and

Wales; their rapid deterioration has meant a wholesale change to the landscape of legal advice.

The effect of LASPO on behind-the-scenes legal work and support services has received little attention from academics, policy makers and the mainstream media, with the notable exception of the Low Commission. Consideration of the impact of LASPO has tended instead to focus on what's happening in the courtroom. Funding for civil representation – that is, legal work done to prepare and represent someone in a civil law court – now stands at around two thirds of its pre-LASPO level (Ministry of Justice and Legal Aid Agency, 2016a). One consequence of these cuts has been a sharp rise in people representing themselves in court, so-called litigants in person. In some 78% of family law cases heard in our courts in 2016, one or both of the litigants were without legal representation (Ministry of Justice, 2016a: 14). To put that into context, it is up from roughly 50% of cases in 2011 (Ministry of Justice, 2016a: 14).

We consider the body of evidence documenting the problems associated with the rise of litigants in person in Chapter Three. By way of summary, the argument runs something like this: when a litigant represents herself in the courtroom, there is a greater chance that paperwork will be missing, incomplete or contain fundamental errors; that the judge will need to intervene or halt proceedings; and the case put forward will not adhere to legal argumentation. All of these factors can slow down and lengthen proceedings. It is these visible, measurable effects of legal aid reform that have received most attention from academics and policy advisors. Given less consideration are the more subtle and long-term effects of the rise of litigants in person on the meaning and operation of justice. This book hopes to go some way towards addressing this gap. It also argues for the need to take a broader, more litigant-focused approach to understanding the impact of legal aid reform, and it is that to which we briefly turn now.

'Lost in process – help needed'

Online forums for those seeking advice on becoming a litigant in person – or 'self-repping', as forum-users refer to it – give some insight into how deeply confusing, stressful and demoralising the experience can be. Wikivorce is one such forum, founded in 2007 by a charitable organisation and promoted by the government in a bid to bolster alternative sources of advice for separating couples. Self-representation is so central to the experience of going through the family court system today that it has its own message board on the forum. The threads tell stories of resilience and mutual support. There are those who have found the forms straightforward enough, those who have been through it and want to help others, as well as useful bits of information from the knowledgeable site administrators.

More plentiful, though, are the messages that reflect a sense of frustration and worry, and in some cases utter panic. 'It's near-idiotic to represent yourself in court', comments a barrister in a newspaper article for *The Guardian*; 'if you can avoid it, you should' (Myers, 2016). The posts from self-reppers on Wikivorce largely accord with this sentiment. A frequent complaint is that there are too many forms, many designed for a pre-LASPO era where solicitors filled them in and knew what level of detail was needed. Forms are returned – sometimes weeks after submission – if they're filled in incorrectly. A common source of complaint is the letters from an ex-partner's solicitor, which, in self-reppers' minds, are incomprehensibly obnoxious. Court orders frequently seem unreasonable and illogical. Why should someone who doesn't own the old family home have to pay for its valuation? And some self-reppers learn the hard way that adhering to a court order isn't voluntary. There are various frustrated exchanges about admissible evidence. These tend to revolve around a deep-seated sense of unfairness that what a self-repper knows in an intuitive sense to be true simply won't stand up in a court of law or, even more jarringly, might be deemed irrelevant. It's like learning a whole new language, one self-repper comments. It's an astute observation. After all, Law isn't a compulsory subject in schools in England and Wales.

This is the world of the self-repper, where legal rules and decisions are often inscrutable and defy the logic of everyday reason and morality. A world where so much is 'lost in the process', to borrow from the forum-user quoted in the title of this section. And, of course, Wikivorce is the world of the relatively well-informed, well-to-do self-repper preparing for court. Rarely do we see posts from those who have completed proceedings or those with complicated cases. For litigants with learning difficulties, or whose first language isn't English, or who lack the skills to do the paperwork – for these social groups, and so many others besides – the problems of self-representation are amplified. All this begs the question: who is fighting legal aid reform?

#Fight4LegalAid

A number of groups have mounted campaigns against the cuts to legal aid. The most notable of these are the Justice Alliance, formed with the express purpose of challenging the reforms, the Legal Action Group, an organisation founded in 1972 to promote access to justice, and the Law Society, which launched its Access to Justice campaign to raise awareness of the recent cuts. All have been highly active in protesting the changes to legal aid and have mounted a coherent critique focusing mainly on the impact of the cuts to equality of access. None of these campaigns, however, have received much mainstream media coverage. Instead, the media debate about legal aid reform has been dominated by politicians and, to a lesser degree, groups of criminal law practitioners. The Criminal Law Solicitors' Association, London Criminal Courts Solicitors' Association, and Criminal Bar Association have been particularly central contributors, having taken to the streets to protest legal aid reform in the summer of 2012 and staged walkouts in 2013 and 2015. Much of the news reporting on the reforms has been focused on these organisations concerns, and particularly the proposal to introduce price-competitive tendering for the allocation of legal aid contracts and to further cut criminal barristers' fees. And the latter issue is the one that newspapers have tended to lead with. A brief look at newspaper headlines on the topic of legal aid reveals that this is the dominant framing in the media, much to the annoyance of campaign groups.

The more striking observation to make here, though, is that news coverage of the reforms has been really very slender. During the last five years (2011-16) there have been just under 1,400 articles in UK national newspapers concerning legal aid reform, with over a fifth of this coverage appearing in the left-liberal newspaper *The Guardian*. Compare this to news coverage of the proposed changes to junior doctors' contracts. In the past *two* years (2015-16), there have been some 2,500 news items about this issue in UK national newspapers. That's roughly 80% more articles in less than half the time.

How can we account for the relative lack of media interest in legal aid reform? It's tempting to suggest that the problem is the opaqueness of our legal system and the related difficulty lay people might have in understanding how legal aid works. But junior doctors' contracts and the organisation of the medical establishment are no less complex. Where the plight of junior doctors does differ to that of legal practitioners is in public support, both for doctors as a professional group, and for the NHS as an institution. In fact, the focus in news reports on criminal lawyers' fees is by no small degree related to the resonance of the cultural stereotype of the 'fat cat' lawyer. Successive Lord Chancellors have drawn on precisely this idea to argue that the problem of legal aid is one of wealthy lawyers not doing their bit and taking on a sufficiently generous volume of *pro bono* work (see for example Gove, 2016). Research carried out by the Legal Action Group suggests that the government has consciously pushed this line in the media by implying that the highest-earning legal aid lawyers represent the norm, rather than the exception (Legal Action Group, 2014: 5). What makes this all the more frustrating is that there is a rich tradition of activism and research around the issue of access to justice. There is, in other words, a way of assessing legal aid reform that shifts the parameters of the debate away from 'fat cat' lawyers and considers the impact on those accessing justice. We turn now to consider this set of ideas.

Legal aid as access to justice

Most liberal democracies introduced a system of publicly funded legal aid in the mid-20th century. The shift from a patchwork provision of charitably funded legal aid to publicly funded support was intimately connected to the rise of the 'access to justice' movement. This global movement was founded on the idea that all members of society should have access to legal advice and advocacy. This idea first took root in post-fascist regimes and the new welfare states of Europe in the aftermath of the Second World War. Then, during the mid-1960s, it took hold in Australia and North America as the counter-cultural revolution sparked a new interest in civil rights (Garth and Capelletti, 1978). The historical-cultural context is crucial. The mid-20th century access to justice movement was centrally concerned with creating a mechanism whereby newly enshrined human rights could be meaningfully defended. Of fundamental importance to this project was the ability for all individuals to access justice, irrespective of background or personal characteristics. Moreover, as Peysner (2014) and Luban (1988) point out, once the state had taken on the role of guaranteeing people's safety and wellbeing, it logically had a responsibility to equip them with the ability to pursue disputes. By contrast, Garth and Capelletti (1978) point out that in the liberal bourgeois nation states of the 18th and 19th century, access to justice was part of an individualistic philosophy of rights whereby the state bore no particular responsibility to intervene in the individual's pursuit of legal remedy. Thus, they point to a historical shift in the mid-20th century whereby access to justice came to refer to *effective*, rather than *formal* equality (Garth and Capelletti, 1978: 183).

Thinking about legal aid in the context of the mid-20th century access to justice movement should prompt us to see this form of support as a thoroughly modern arrangement that answers to the distinct needs of the liberal democratic state, as much as the needs of individual citizens. This is not to suggest that the access to justice movement has been consistently positive about publicly funded legal aid. Indeed, since the 1970s it has become increasingly focused on non-legal approaches to dispute resolution and, as such, the function and importance of legal aid has been called into question (Capelletti and Garth, 1981: 4). Arguments of this sort tend to advance two main points of contention. First, that access to justice isn't simply about what happens in the courtroom, but rather involves entrenched barriers to justice that disadvantage particular social groups. As Goriely and Paterson put it:

> We now recognise that the health of a nation depends much more crucially on good diet and clean water than on medical intervention. Equally, a just society is much more likely to depend on fair allocation of jobs, education, housing, and income than on anything a legal aid scheme can deliver (Goriely and Paterson, 1996: 7).

The second, and perhaps more damning, criticism is that the commitment to legal aid ignores the problems with formal dispute resolution processes. The crux of this argument lies in the idea that '[u]nfair laws are still unfair even when they are strictly enforced through superb legal aid schemes' (Goriely and Paterson, 1996: 7).

Thus, if the mid-20th-century access to justice movement interrogated the meaning of 'access', the post-1970s movement has focused on the meaning of 'justice', suggesting that we should look beyond legal definitions and processes. This set of ideas has had a significant impact on policy, giving rise to what Genn calls an 'anti-litigation/anti-adjudication rhetoric' (Genn, 2010: 4). Lord Woolf's (1996) 'Access to Justice' review is particularly important here, as well as the subsequent Modernising Justice white paper (Lord Chancellor's Office, 1998) and Access to Justice Act 1999. In these influential access to justice reforms, the task of civil advocacy is reframed so that litigants are urged to treat the court as a remedy of last resort and fully explore alternative methods of dispute resolution.

There is much to recommend in this holistic approach to access to justice, not least its recognition that a court hearing is one event in a potentially long history of injustice and that the legal system can produce and deepen social harm. It is, though, an approach that is easily misappropriated. The Ministry of Justice's (2010) green paper on legal aid reform and subsequent review of the accompanying consultation demonstrate as much. This argues for the retrenchment of civil legal services on the basis that legal dispute is simply one of various forms of dispute and a blunt instrument for certain types of problem. Similarly, the suggestion that what people really lack is access to non-legal forms of dispute resolution becomes an argument for cutting funding to support legal remedy.

It's easy to interpret this as a simple case of instrumental politics, but it's important to recognise that the disavowal of legal dispute and adjudication has helped create a mood that is unsympathetic to legal aid. And it is of particular concern that this move away from court-based dispute resolution has not eventuated in an expansion of out-of-court support and advice. Far from it. As mentioned earlier, it is civil legal advice that has been particularly affected by the cuts. As an aside, it's worth pointing out that, historically, this behind-the-scenes legal support has kept people from taking their dispute to court just as much as it has directed those heading down the formal pathway to justice. 'Any lawyer worth their salt will tell…you that it is far better to avoid coming to court if you can', points out Lucy Reed, in a popular self-help book for those looking to represent themselves in a family court (Reed, 2014: 1). It's a view held by many family lawyers, but what's involved in getting people to resolve a complaint outside of the courtroom is little understood – even, it seems, by those making decisions about legal aid provision.

In line with a holistic conception of access to justice, this book is particularly interested in the out-of-courtroom work that lawyers do as counsellors, advocates (with a small 'a') and advisors. In line with traditional ideas about access to justice, we see this as a service that legal aid can – and indeed, did and should – provide. We also hold firm to the idea that all members of a society should have equal access to legal advice, the courtroom and adjudication. This is not to ignore the significant problems with our legal system and lawyer-led dispute resolution. It is simply to acknowledge that making traditional legal routes to justice unaffordable to most entrenches inequality, especially in a social context where more and more disputes are settled judicially. At the time of writing, newspaper headlines are focused on legal action being brought against the government's response to the Brexit referendum and against the Labour party for changing its rules on political party members' voting rights. The cuts to legal aid don't thwart litigiousness: they simply mean that some people are disallowed access to the law when pursuing justice.

Structure of the book

Chapter Two outlines the historical and international context for the recent reforms to legal aid in England and Wales. We recall that legal aid was originally conceived as a form of social welfare with near-universal eligibility and outline a shift away from this conception. We also examine international comparators to the legal aid system in England and Wales. Thinking about legal aid in international perspective reveals not just a significant difference in the level of state spending on this form of welfare, but also the role of legal aid in a broader set of institutional arrangements.

Chapter Three reviews the evidence about the impact of the recent reforms to legal aid in England and Wales, drawing on a wide range of literature from the Legal Aid Agency, Ministry of Justice, Magistrates Association, Low Commission, Select Committees and academic researchers. We pay particular attention to research on the rise of litigants in person. We end the chapter by pointing out that much research in this area is focused on directly measurable factors, such as trial-length and formal legal outcomes. The question of how litigants' experiences of justice might be affected by the lack of publicly funded advocacy is unaddressed in existing work; indeed a Ministry of Justice-commissioned review of the reforms pointed to this very omission (Trinder et al, 2014).

Chapter Four argues that the current conception of legal aid neglects the broad spectrum of work that lawyers do to help resolve disputes. We put forward an alternative conception that recognises the role of legal aid lawyers as interpreters of the law, counsellors, advisors and go-betweens, as well as formal legal representatives. To make our case, we draw on insights from the Civil and Social Justice Panel Survey which, among other things, illuminates the role of lawyers in facilitating justice, both in a technical sense and in terms of litigants' overall experience of justice.

The final chapter of the book, Chapter Five, brings together the various strands of our discussion and suggests that the recent reforms reduce the role of the lawyer in dispute-resolution, and with little consideration for the consequences of such a shift. We suggest that the debate about legal aid reform should be refocused around four key issues: the social value of legal aid, the impact of the reforms on unassisted litigants' experience of justice, a systems approach to legal aid spending, and the impact of legal aid cuts on the legal system.

2

LEGAL AID REFORM IN HISTORICAL AND INTERNATIONAL PERSPECTIVE

Legal aid, broadly-conceived, has a long history. As Pollock notes, help to cover the costs of legal dispute 'has existed as long as the law itself' (Pollock, 1975: 9). He's thinking, in the main, about the charitable and often ad hoc support provided by lawyers. Statutory protections date back to an Act passed in 1495 that allowed Justices in the superior courts to order legal advocates to advise and represent litigants who lacked the means to pay (Pollock, 1975: 10). Special provision was made in criminal courts, where a system of 'dock briefs' operated, meaning that any robed barrister could be called upon in court to offer cheap representation to an unassisted person (Roshier and Teff, 2013). The late 19th and early 20th century also saw the growth of voluntary services providing legal aid, most notably 'poor man's lawyers', who offered free legal support to people living in impoverished areas of London (Leat, 1975).

In short, subsidised, charitable and free support for legal dispute resolution has existed for centuries. Until the mid-20th century, though, it was largely inadequate, depending upon judges to intervene and direct assistance, and lawyers to shoulder the cost of advocacy. Provision was of inconsistent quality, directed at the very poor, and subject to regional variation. The creation of a modern legal aid system in the post-Second World War period was directed at changing all this. This chapter examines the emergence of publicly funded legal aid in England and Wales, considers its historical development and then places it in international context.

The early years of the legal aid scheme in England and Wales

In Chapter One we discussed the mid-20th century access to justice movement, noting its focus on meaningful equality of access to legal remedy, as opposed to formal equality before the law. It is no surprise that this idea took root in the then-emerging welfare regimes of northern Europe and the post-fascist regimes of southern Europe. It is in such political climates that publicly funded legal aid first emerged (Garth and Capelletti, 1978). It did so partly because it answered to the practical problems of charitable provision touched on earlier and, more importantly, because it chimed with – indeed, expressed – the idea that the state's principal role lay in advancing the opportunities and wellbeing of its citizens.

A chief task of this new political agenda was to create mechanisms to enable equality of treatment, care and provision. In the UK this involved, among other things, the creation of a national health service, free at the point of access; state-administered financial support for people who were unemployed, sick and disabled; and publicly funded civil legal aid. As a brief aside, it's worth noting there were earlier statutory provisions for criminal legal aid, first in the Criminal Appeal Act 1907, which provided publicly funded support for those in criminal appeal hearings, and then in a set of Acts in the early 1930s that introduced criminal legal aid to those in the lower courts (Pollock, 1975: 21-2). Riven with problems – including strict eligibility rules and dependence on the court to administer support – criminal legal aid didn't become a properly-functioning scheme until the mid-1960s (Ward and Akhtar, 2011: 412).

To return to our main point of interest here: it was during the mid-20th century period of welfare state-building that the first steps were taken to create a workable system of publicly funded civil legal aid in England and Wales. The time was right for such a development. Not only was there growing public support for sounder social welfare arrangements, but the rapid increase in divorce during the Second World War had drawn attention to gaps in existing forms of support. The Rushcliffe Committee was set up to offer solutions to the problem. It reported to Parliament in 1945 and set out a clear case for radical change, noting that 'a service which was at best somewhat patchy has become totally inadequate' (Rushcliffe Committee, 1945: 23, para 126). The Committee's report received cross-party support and its recommendations were introduced in the Legal Advice and Assistance Act 1949. The Act provided the blueprint for a comprehensive, publicly funded civil legal aid system, the first of its kind in the world (Pollock 1975: 17). The Law Society was given responsibility for administering the scheme, and this professional body remained in charge of things for some forty years.

Though today it very rarely features in discussions of the mid-20th century turn towards welfarism, at the time, the civil legal aid scheme was conceived as 'one of the great pillars of the post-war welfare state', as Lord Beecham recently put it (Beecham in HL Deb, 19 May 2011: Col 1535). It's of particular note that the Rushcliffe Committee and subsequent Act conceived civil legal aid as a service available to a wide income group. The aspiration – like so many other welfare initiatives of this period – was to offer a nationwide service to help meet the costs of legal dispute for all but the most affluent. Hence the scheme used a sliding scale of contributions, with the very poor paying nothing towards the cost of litigation and middle-earners paying something. Thus, when the scheme was introduced in 1950, 80% of the population was eligible for free or subsidised legal representation in the higher courts (Roshier and Teff 2013: 190).

All of this represented a huge step forwards in the creation of a modern legal aid system. Not that the benefits accrued immediately. In fact, the 1949 Act was implemented cautiously, and it took a full decade for its vision to be in any way realised. Funding had been left uncapped so as to enable equal access. To alleviate anxiety about spiralling costs, the scheme was implemented in a piecemeal fashion (Pollock, 1975: 76-7). Of particular importance was the omission of a legal advisory service, something that the Rushcliffe Committee and

1949 Act had recommended (Hynes and Robins, 2009: 21). Instead, for the first decade, civil legal aid was directed rather narrowly towards litigation and representation. That began to change in 1959 with the creation of the 'pink form' advice scheme, which enabled solicitors to claim from the state a modest fee for up to one and a half hours of oral advice about a particular legal action (Pollock, 1975: 79-80).

Still, there were significant omissions: the 'pink form' scheme didn't cover lawyers' fees for writing letters and clients could only access this support if they were pursuing litigation. So the problem of access to civil legal advice persisted. By the late 1960s, this was becoming a source of concern among campaigners, who increasingly looked at developments in the USA and found the UK civil legal aid system wanting. There, President Johnson's War on Poverty programme had paved the way for the creation of neighbourhood law offices, community-based legal advice centres run by salaried solicitors (Hynes and Robins, 2009: 22). Designed with the aim of bringing a distinctive mix of social and legal support to the heart of impoverished and hard-to-reach communities, neighbourhood law offices signalled a shift in thinking about access to justice, one that was evident in European countries too. No longer a matter of providing in-court advocacy to the poor, access to justice had come to be seen as a matter of social welfare-oriented interventions. In the UK, this set of ideas influenced public opinion and political debate about legal aid, which from the late 1960s focused on the idea that the legal aid scheme was failing to address the 'unmet need' for support (Pollock, 1975: 86). This view was put forward in 'Justice for All', a powerfully written pamphlet published in 1968 by the Society of Labour Lawyers. This set out a vision for reform that involved creating a thoroughgoing legal advisory system in areas where need was particularly high. It received widespread approval from politicians on the left and right (Pollock, 1975: 91-3). Thus, a new political consensus emerged – on the broad principles, if not the finer details – that legal aid was failing those who needed it most (Hynes and Robins, 2009: 22).

This desire for change gave rise to the growth of the not-for-profit legal services sector. Unhindered by rules about eligibility and coverage, such organisations came to play an increasingly central role in responding to the 'unmet need' for legal advice. The Citizens Advice Bureau (CAB) was particularly important in this respect. Formed during the Second World War to provide information to the public, the CAB grew significantly during the late 1960s and 1970s as the legal support and advice it provided expanded (Hynes, 2012: 34-5). Concern about the 'unmet need' for legal advice hastened other developments, most notably the creation of community law centres, modelled on the US neighbourhood law offices. The North Kensington Neighbourhood Law Centre, opened in 1970 in a disadvantaged part of London, was the first of its kind in the UK, though some point to the 'Poor Man's Lawyers' of the late 19th century as an important precursor (Garth, 1980: 53). Its funding initially derived from a mix of charity and local authority support, and its aim was to offer a form of holistic assistance that went beyond legal advice. More than anything else, it aimed to answer to the socio-legal problems and everyday lives of the community that it served (Garth, 1980: 58). The North Kensington Law Centre wasn't without problems and critics, but it kick-started a significant change in community-level legal support, so much so that by 1974 there were 15 such centres in the UK, and by 1976 there were 24 (Garth, 1980: 61-3).

It is in this context that the Legal Advice and Assistance Act 1972 was introduced. Though (again) only implemented in part, the Act significantly extended the existing publicly funded advisory scheme. It was the start of what Hynes and Robins (2009: 26) call a 'golden period' in legal aid provision. Among other things it led to the creation of the 'green form' scheme in 1973, an improved version of the older 'pink form' scheme. The means-tested green form scheme allowed solicitors to offer advice on any matter of law – not just litigation – for the cost of up to two hours of work, and without having to make any formal application (Pollock, 1975: 93). It covered all sorts of legal support, including letter-writing, preparation of cases for employment tribunals, organising and overseeing negotiations, and expert opinion (Kempson, 1989:1). This service quickly became a very significant feature of the legal aid system; by the late 1980s, spending on the green form scheme accounted for roughly a fifth of legal aid expenditure (Kempson, 1989:1).

The first few decades of publicly funded legal aid were, then, characterised by slow expansion of services and concerns about the delivery and scope of legal advice. One debate that kept resurfacing was the question of whether legal aid providers should be salaried by the state or private contractors. For some – predominantly those supportive of the Law Centre movement – the argument for having salaried legal aid lawyers was clear: it would allow legal aid to encompass a wide range of support and would help control costs. Moreover, salaried solicitors' offices could meet a gap in provision by offering advice on social welfare law, an area that private law firms have historically neglected. They prefer instead to specialise in family and criminal law where there is the opportunity for both a private and publicly funded client base (Hynes, 2012: 26-7). For others, the idea of salaried lawyers was anathema to the vision of the Rushcliffe Committee report and 1949 Act. Here, there was clear emphasis on the importance of publicly funded lawyers retaining their professional independence and providing a service of the same quality as that received by fee-paying clients (Pollock, 1975: 6-7). As Peysner (2014) notes, such a view reflected Cold War suspicion about the perils of state-controlled legal services.

In the event, legal aid in England and Wales became (and has remained) a service provided predominantly by private law firms and not-for-profit organisations in receipt of government funding – the 'judicare' system, as it's sometimes called. Today, debates about the merits and problems with this arrangement – about, on the one hand, evenness of provision and the role of legal support, and on the other hand, quality of service and professional independence – are no longer central. Instead, the focus in policy and public debate has shifted towards seeing legal aid as an unnecessarily costly service that suffers from a lack of government oversight and control. We will examine the impact of this significant change in focus in more detail in due course, but first consider the start of this shift in thinking.

Disorganisation and reorganisation: legal aid reform in the 1980s and 1990s

By the mid-1980s, the publicly funded legal aid scheme had grown to incorporate a wide range of services. Particularly significant was the growth in the criminal legal aid scheme. The Police and Criminal Evidence Act 1984 introduced the right for those detained at police stations to receive publicly funded legal advice. By this point, duty schemes had also been introduced in police stations and magistrates' courts, allowing those detained under the criminal law to receive free legal support from a solicitor in these sites (Hynes and Robins, 2009: 26-7). This, along with the growth of the civil legal system during the 1970s, meant that 'by 1986 legal aid represented 11 per cent of solicitors' incomes (an increase of 5 per cent in ten years)' (Hynes and Robins, 2009: 27).

As the legal aid system grew, so did organisational problems and concerns about overspending. By the mid-1980s there had been an evident shift in the terms of the debate, due partly to broader political concerns about the rapid expansion of the welfare state. The then Conservative government ordered an Efficiency Scrutiny Team to review legal aid expenditure (Kempson, 1989: 2). The results were startling, revealing a 50% increase in legal aid spending between 1984 and 1986, a hike in the budget that couldn't be explained entirely by an increase in casework (Hynes and Robins, 2009: 28). Concerns about misuse of legal aid funds arose, with the relatively unregulated green form scheme becoming a particular focus for scrutiny. In sharp contrast to the political consensus of the late 1960s and 1970s, legal aid had, by the late 1980s, come to be reframed as a problem of overuse and lack of government scrutiny.

The Conservative government saw an opportunity to radically reform the legal aid scheme in England and Wales. First, it dramatically reduced eligibility, and then – after its re-election in 1987 – it implemented the Legal Aid Act 1988. The Act sought to harmonise the legal aid scheme by bringing criminal legal aid and civil legal aid under the remit of the same operating body. It did so by shifting responsibility for legal aid administration from the Law Society to the newly-created Legal Aid Board (LAB), a non-departmental public body. The organisational change was widely perceived – for good and for ill – as an attempt to loosen the profession's control of the legal aid scheme. Certainly, once the LAB had taken over, it moved towards a more managerial approach to providing legal aid (Hynes 2012: 29). One key innovation was the introduction of a 'franchising' scheme whereby solicitors' firms were given funding priority if they successfully passed an assessment that guaranteed a certain standard of service (Hynes, 2012: 30). It was the start of the move towards contracting – but more on that later.

The overall aim of the 1988 Act was to bring legal aid spending under control. On that count, it failed miserably. Spending continued to creep upwards throughout the 1990s. In response, the LAB further tightened the eligibility rules on income and capital, making it, by the end of the decade, 'largely a sink service for people on means-tested benefits' (Hynes and Robins, 2009: 30). The seemingly unstoppable growth of legal aid provision came to be taken as an indication that far-reaching reform was needed.

It is in this context that Lord Woolf undertook his 'Access to Justice' review, directed towards creating a set of overarching rules for civil procedure. Woolf's primary concern was to tackle the 'excessive' costs of the civil justice system on the basis that this restricted access to middle-earners who now found themselves ineligible for legal aid (Woolf, 1996: Chapter 7, para 11). His final report took legal aid reform to be a key means of implementing wholesale change and, within this, controlling lawyers' fees was seen as paramount (Woolf, 1996). Woolf doesn't directly accuse lawyers of escalating costs, but it's nonetheless clear that they are seen here as part of the problem, and not just in terms of their dependence on public funds. The new landscape of civil litigation set out by Woolf (1996) starts from the principle that court proceedings should be a last resort and alternative forms of dispute resolution are, in most cases, preferable. The underlying premise here is that too many disputes are lawyer-led and end in the courtroom.

In Woolf's review we find a set of ideas that would become highly influential and pave the way for legal aid reform in the 21st century. The 'Legal Aid – Targeting Need' green paper (Legal Aid Board, 1995), published in the same year as Woolf's interim report, largely shared its vision and recommended that non-legal services should be eligible for legal aid funding. The Family Law Act 1996 made this a reality by introducing public funding for mediation in some family law cases (Liebmann, 2011: 33).

This shift in thinking was well-received by the New Labour government. A year after coming to office in 1997, it published the 'Modernising Justice' white paper, which set out a vision for an at-once expanded advisory service and a slimmed-down scheme (Lord Chancellor's Office, 1998). This model of concomitant expansion and contraction would be achieved, the paper suggested, by redirecting services to those who needed them most. It was an idea that harked back to the earlier debate about the 'unmet need' for legal aid; indeed, Lord Irvine, the then Lord Chancellor, even used the phrase in his press statement launching the white paper (BBC, 1998). Servicing the unmet need required savings to be made. In an echo of Woolf, the white paper suggested promoting alternative forms of dispute resolution on the basis that they discouraged unnecessary litigation and would, over time, reduce the overall cost of the legal aid scheme.

The white paper provided the basis for the Access to Justice Act 1999. Coming into effect in 2000, the Act instigated wide-reaching reform. The central aim was to establish and consolidate core business. Thus, for the first time, certain areas of law were removed from scope, including conveyancing, personal injury (except in clinical negligence cases), boundary disputes and defamation (House of Commons Justice Committee, 2011). The merits test that had previously been used to determine if a matter warranted legal aid – a relatively simple matter of there being reasonable legal grounds to proceed – was replaced with a Funding Code. The new Code meant that funding was restricted to cases where there was a good chance of success and costs were unlikely to exceed the damages awarded (Zander, 2000: 14-5). Moreover, a hard cap was introduced to legal aid spending, something first suggested by the previous administration in a 1995 green paper (Lord Chancellor's Office, 1995).[1] As criminal legal aid provision was mainly protected by Article 6 of the European Convention on Human Rights, it was the civil legal aid budget that was particularly affected by the cap. Lord Irvine was explicit about this, indicating in a House of Lords debate that the civil legal aid budget would be 'what is left over out of the budget after the requirements of criminal legal aid have been met' (in Paterson, 2011: 90).

The Access to Justice Act 1999 also brought another change in governing body. The Legal Aid Board was replaced with the Legal Services Commission (LSC), and the Lord Chancellor was given direct control over the composition of its board. The LSC was then given responsibility for the new Criminal Defence Service and the Community Legal Service, essentially splitting the organisation of civil and criminal legal aid. The core aim of the Community Legal Service was to investigate local need and direct community support, matching supply to demand (Hynes, 2012: 55). Its flagship policy was to create regional partnerships (so-called Community Legal Services Partnerships) that coordinated different service providers and local authorities (Hynes, 2012: 55). As part of this reorganisation of services, the green form scheme was relabelled the Legal Help scheme and alternative forms of dispute resolution – notably family mediation – were eligible for funding from the mainstream legal aid budget (Hynes, 2012: 57).

Once the LSC was operational, it took a number of steps to shore up the quality of provision and stem costs. Of particular importance were the extension of the franchising scheme and the introduction of block contracts. Rolled out in stages between 2000 and 2003, the franchising scheme made it compulsory for civil legal aid suppliers to possess a quality mark in a particular area of law and provision (Zander, 2000: 13). One aim was to concentrate legal aid supply. Paterson (2011: 94) explains this in terms of the LSC's discovery that around '70 per cent of the profession [was doing] 30 per cent of the legal aid work'. The LSC therefore concluded that a significant proportion of providers were 'dabblers and likely to be doing the work inefficiently'

(Paterson, 2011: 94). Franchising set out to change this by encouraging the consolidation of legal aid work. It wasn't without problems. Law firms providing wide-ranging and general legal advice – small rural solicitors' offices, for example – were significantly disadvantaged by the new terms of the scheme. A knock-on effect of franchising was a sharp decrease in the volume of suppliers of legal aid, down from roughly 11,000 to 5,000 (Paterson, 2011: 94). Moreover, providers had to bid for blocks of contracts that allowed them a set number of 'matter starts' for legal advice. The introduction of the cap meant that the allocation could only be exceeded with the LSC's approval. This was rarely given, and thus some firms dealing with high-growth areas, such as immigration, reported having to turn eligible clients away (Manson, 2012).

Legal aid reform in the 21st century: the cost agenda

The Access to Justice reforms were highly ambitious, directed as they were towards rationalising and consolidating the legal aid scheme so that services could be redirected towards those most in need. The Community Legal Service struggled to put this into practice, and by the mid-2000s the set of regional partnerships that were supposed to play a key role in linking demand and supply were deemed ineffective and duly closed (Hynes, 2012: 61-2). To boot, the reforms had done nothing to halt the overall growth of legal aid spending. In the opening decade of the 21st century this increasingly came to be seen as the overriding issue. In 2005 Lord Falconer, then Lord Chancellor, commissioned Lord Carter of Coles to review the procurement process for legal aid, with the aim of achieving a predictable rate of spending by 2010/11. Of particular concern to Falconer was the increase in criminal aid expenditure during the 1990s and 2000s. Falconer's 2005 report, 'A Fairer Deal for Legal Aid', noted that spending had increased from £1.5 billion to £2 billion between 1997 and 2004, but, he added, 'there has been a disproportionate growth, over the same period, in the criminal legal aid spend (up 37%), compared to legal advice and representation in civil and family matters, including asylum (down 24%)' (Department of Constitutional Affairs, 2005: 4).

Two key factors explain much of the increase in criminal legal aid spending during this period. First, an increase in proceeded criminal cases, and secondly an increase in serious criminal cases requiring an extended period of legal support and representation (Cape and Moorhead, 2005). Crucially, the costs related to the latter were transferred to the legal aid budget in 2003; before that, expenditure for legal aid provision for Crown and higher court cases was covered by the HM Courts and Tribunals Service (Hynes and Robins, 2009: 49). Moreover, the expense of the high-cost cases heard at these courts grew rapidly during the first decade of the 21st century, so much so that in 2005/6 spending on this small set of criminal cases accounted for roughly a third of the overall legal aid budget (Hynes and Robins, 2009: 49).

The key point here is that the rising bill for criminal legal aid – much of it a knock-on effect of reorganisation and legislative activity – had begun to impinge on civil legal aid spending, a situation exacerbated by the introduction of a hard cap on expenditure in the late 1990s. Indeed, Stephen Orchard, on leaving his post as Chief Executive of the LSC, commented that the rising cost of the criminal legal aid scheme constituted the most significant threat to the civil legal aid scheme (Orchard, 2003).

Carter's (2006) review of the procurement process for legal aid aimed to create solutions to this situation. In making recommendations for reform, he took particular aim at criminal legal aid scheme spending. He suggested, among other things, introducing fixed and graduated fees for duty solicitors in both police stations and Magistrates' courts, the restriction of fees for Crown Court cases, and, most controversially, that a system of best-value tendering should be introduced for high cost criminal cases and almost all civil contracts. This was to involve legal aid suppliers entering into competitive tendering to win a contract for provision. The attractiveness of a marketised system lay in its the potential to encourage suppliers to do more for less; it seemed to meet the need for cost-efficiency on the one hand, and quality control on the other. The plans met fierce resistance from lawyers and their various professional bodies and best-value tendering was eventually abandoned shortly before the 2010 election. The idea didn't go away though. Chris Grayling, the Lord Chancellor for the subsequent Coalition government, resurrected plans for competitive tendering in the form of dual contracting, which were duly shelved indefinitely by his successor Michael Gove (Gove, 2016).

Carter's (2006) recommendation that lawyers' hourly fees should be replaced by fixed fees did make it through, though. This came into effect in 2007 for civil legal aid and then, despite some setbacks due to opposition from professional groups, for criminal legal aid in 2008 (Hynes, 2012: 65-7). The year also brought a global economic downturn. In the face of cross-department spending reductions, the case for further reducing legal aid fees was difficult to resist. In 2010, Jack Straw, then Lord Chancellor, introduced a programme of staged cuts to fees for work in the Crown and higher courts (Hynes, 2012: 73). The move infuriated many in the legal profession, who pointed out that the growth in legal aid expenditure was not tied to inflated fees. Instead, they pointed out – as we have done earlier – that much of the growth in spending was due to an increase in serious criminal casework caused, more than anything else, by changes to criminal justice policy and practice (Cape and Moorhead, 2005; LECG, 2006).

In fact, the move to curtail criminal legal aid fees was only partially about reducing costs. Straw's introduction of staged cuts was also aimed at reducing the ranks of criminal lawyers because, to his mind, the UK had become 'over-lawyered' (2009: 5). Never mind that New Labour had overseen the introduction of an extraordinarily high number of new criminal laws (Reiner, 2007). The problem, for Straw and others besides, wasn't too many laws, but too many lawyers. This should give us pause to reconsider the reforms New Labour undertook in the first decade of the 21st century. The extension of franchising and the introduction of (and then reduction in) fixed fees made legal aid work financially unviable for small providers, while larger organisations increasingly sought to offset the cost of legal aid work by undertaking private work in more lucrative areas of law (Jackson, 2010). Looked at in this way, the cost agenda in legal aid reform was directed as much towards reshaping the legal sector as it was towards reducing spending.

The retrenchment of civil legal aid

In 2010 the Conservative-LibDem Coalition government started a five-year period in office. The new Lord Chancellor, Kenneth Clarke, shared with his predecessor an understanding of legal aid as a problem of glut and overuse. In making a case for reform he was significantly helped by the fact that the Conservative party had come to power on the basis that they would make deep cuts to social welfare services. As part of its austerity programme, the government ordered the Ministry of Justice to make £2 billion of savings per annum from 2014/15 (Cookson, 2011: 6). A sharp reduction to legal aid spending was on the cards. It's worth noting a global pattern here. A number of economically-developed countries have latterly undertaken cuts to legal aid under the banner of austerity politics. In Australia and the USA, for example, there has been a sharp reduction in federal legal aid spending in the five years to 2016. These cuts have become particularly contentious in Australia, where Community Legal Centres – Australia's equivalent of Law Centres – are due to have their funding reduced by AUS $12.1 million in July 2017 (Law Council of Australia, 2016). Programmes of cuts have also been undertaken in New Zealand and Northern Ireland, but the focus has been on cutting lawyers' fees. In reducing spending in England and Wales, Clarke took similar steps. On taking office, he took up Straw's programme of staged cuts and introduced a 10% cut to civil legal aid fees.

In other ways, the Coalition government's reforms took a radical departure both from the previous administration's programme of change and the austerity-related reforms undertaken in other jurisdictions. Most notably, the Coalition government focused its attention on the retrenchment of the civil legal aid scheme. The 2010 green paper, published within a year of the Coalition government coming to office, gives due warning of this development (Ministry of

Justice, 2010). The Ministerial foreword gives a flavour of the report's overall approach:

> The current [legal aid] scheme bears very little resemblance to the one that was introduced in 1949. It has expanded, so much so that it is now one of the most expensive in the world, available for a very wide range of issues, including some which should not require any legal expertise to resolve. I believe that this has encouraged people to bring their problems before the courts too readily, even sometimes when the courts are not well placed to provide the best solutions. This has led to the availability of taxpayer funding for unnecessary litigation (Ministry of Justice, 2010: 3).

There's a forceful suggestion here that much legal dispute is unnecessary – and, of course, Clarke is thinking of civil disputes here, rather than criminal matters. It's an idea that echoes Woolf's (1996) suggestion that court hearings need to be reframed as a remedy of 'last resort'. The suggestion would reappear again in the Family Justice Review (Ministry of Justice et al, 2011), published a year after Clarke's green paper. In making the case for a radical reshaping of family law, the review takes mediation to be a central means of deterring people from using litigation. In Clarke's interpretation of the problem, the issue is squarely one of individuals coming to courts 'too readily' because the taxpayer is footing the bill. Litigiousness, here, is an individual character flaw, rather than a societal problem. Following this logic, the solution to overuse of the courtroom is a simple one: remove people's access, and they'll be forced to revert to other means of dispute resolution. Supply, in other words, would lead demand.

This set of ideas informed the Legal Aid, Sentencing and Punishing of Offenders Act 2012 (LASPO), which came into effect in April 2013. In some senses the Act represents an extension of previous reforms. For example, the Act replaced the LSC with the Legal Aid Agency, making it an executive agency of the Ministry of Justice and giving the Lord Chancellor direct oversight. In doing so, LASPO effectively finished a 15-year process of bringing the legal aid scheme under closer government scrutiny. And, as with previous Acts, LASPO aimed to cut costs. Previous administrations had done so as a means of tackling the problem of unpredictable growth in spending. As a number of commentators point out, expenditure had reached an even keel by the mid-2000s (Cookson, 2011; Paterson, 2009). Not that this mattered anymore: by 2010, the case for a new mode of austerity politics seemed undeniable. The Coalition government duly changed the terms of the debate and argued that, even at a steady rate of spending, the legal aid scheme was simply *too expensive.* And where previous administrations had sought to use the savings from cuts to legal aid to bolster services where the need was greatest – notably New Labour's Access to Justice Act 1999 – the only significant system-change implemented by LASPO was a planned increase in legal aid spending on mediation. The Family and Children Act 2013 introduced a push on demand for such services by making mediation compulsory for all divorcing couples embarking on court proceedings.

The Coalition's reforms to legal aid were, then, directed towards cutting services for the sake of making an overall saving – £350 million, to be precise (Hynes, 2012: 90). Roughly a third of the savings would be found by cutting lawyers' fees. There was to be a 10% cut to all civil legal aid fees, and a staggered 17% cut in fees for most suppliers of criminal legal aid (which was later abandoned after the first 8.75% reduction to fees was introduced in 2014) (McGuinness, 2016: 11). Further economies were to be achieved by introducing a mandatory telephone gateway service to provide initial legal advice on debt, special educational needs, and discrimination where there was a suspected breach of the Equality Act 2010 (Ministry of Justice and Legal Aid Agency, 2016b: 7).

By far the biggest saving, though, was to be made by taking many areas of civil law out of scope, amounting, the Ministry of Justice estimated, to a £279 million reduction in annual spending (Hynes, 2012: 90). Most matters related to immigration, housing, welfare benefits, debt and employment were taken out of scope, as were divorce and private law children cases, historically the biggest areas of civil law. An exception was made for those who could provide evidence that they had been victims of domestic violence. This proved to be an inadequate protection, as indicated by research by the Rights of Women et al (2014). Their online survey of 182 female victims of domestic violence found that, even after the government relaxed the rules concerning domestic violence evidence and legal aid eligibility, 38% of respondents did not have the mandatory evidence to receive publicly funded legal assistance (Rights of Women et al, 2014).

Such research suggests that LASPO restricts access to justice, and in such a way as to disadvantage already-disadvantaged social groups. By way of answer to concerns about inequality of access, and to ensure compliance with Article 6 of the European Convention on Human Rights, LASPO incorporated an 'Exceptional Case Funding' caveat. First introduced in the Access to Justice Act 1999, this allowed the restrictions in legal aid provision to be overruled on the basis that an individual's human rights would be breached without publicly funded assistance. This mechanism has proven woefully inadequate – but more on that in Chapter Three where we assess the impact of LASPO.

Legal aid in international perspective

As already mentioned, the Coalition government's case for retrenchment was based on the argument that the legal aid scheme in England and Wales had become too expensive. In making this point, politicians and media outlets repeatedly drew comparisons with spending in other countries, and argued that expenditure was significantly higher in England and Wales. Take, by way of example, Clarke's 2010 speech to the Centre for Crime and Justice Studies:

> Our legal aid system has grown to an extent that we spend more than almost anywhere else in the world. France spends £3 per head of the population. Germany; £5. New Zealand, with a comparable legal system, spends £8. In England and Wales, we spend a staggering £38 per head of population (in Grimwood, 2015: 9).

In fact, as the Legal Action Group has pointed out, data from the European Commission for the Efficiency of Justice shows that England and Wales has the third highest level of spending per capita after Norway and Northern Ireland (Hynes, 2014). More importantly, straightforward comparisons of expenditure are deeply misleading (Hynes, 2014).

The same point is made in a study commissioned by the Ministry of Justice (Bowles and Perry, 2009). The report compared legal aid in England and Wales with four other EU countries (France, Sweden, Germany and the Netherlands) and three non-EU countries (Australia, New Zealand and Canada). England and Wales certainly came out with the highest per capita spend, but Bowles and Perry (2009) repeatedly point out that expenditure can only really be understood by examining broader institutional arrangements. They gesture towards a wide range of contextual factors that shape each jurisdiction's spending. For example, Sweden's relatively low rate of legal aid-spending is in part a consequence of the much lower proportion of criminal cases being handled by their court system, relative to jurisdictions like England and Wales (Bowles and Perry, 2009: 14). Another factor is the normalisation of legal insurance schemes in Sweden – as is the case in Germany – a source of legal assistance that often replaces publicly funded assistance for middle-income earners (Bowles and Perry, 2009: 14).

Of particular note is Bowles and Perry's (2009) observation that those jurisdictions with a more inquisitorial justice system, such as the Netherlands, incur lower legal aid costs than England and Wales because they favour mediation as a form of dispute resolution (Bowles and Perry, 2009: 13). We're tempted to add the word 'naturally' here, because the implication is that inquisitorial systems are especially conducive to alternative non-legal forms of dispute resolution. In other words, the success and popularity of the latter might to some degree rely on the former. As an aside here, this suggests that in adversarial jurisdictions, such as England and Wales, there might be entrenched, system-related obstacles to non-legal routes to justice. Woolf (1996) certainly acknowledges this, but the recent reforms have ignored such matters.

Bowles and Perry (2009) also note that courtrooms in inquisitorial jurisdictions are better resourced. The same point is made by Dannemann (1996) in a review of legal aid provision in Germany and England and Wales. Litigants that make it to this stage of the legal process in these jurisdictions tend to benefit from well-equipped courtrooms and clerks. Put differently, and as Hynes (2014) points out, the level of *indirect* legal assistance for the individual litigant is higher in inquisitorial systems than in adversarial systems like that of England and Wales. We might think of this in terms of a premium that goes some way towards offsetting the need for direct legal assistance. For example, in Bowles and Perry's (2009) analysis, Sweden's legal aid spending was a relatively low €10.57 per capita, while England and Wales spent a relatively high €57.87 per capita. When we look at spending on courts, however, this gap is reversed, with Sweden devoting €51.32 per capita and England and Wales spending €8.09 per capita (Bowles and Perry, 2009: 27).

Thinking along these lines should prompt us to reconsider how the problem of legal aid has been conceived by the UK government. For one thing, we should recognise that legal aid is just one source of publicly funded legal assistance for litigants. We spend a very considerable amount on *direct* assistance, but a relatively low amount on *indirect* forms of assistance. Other countries strike a different balance. In fact, since Bowles and Perry's (2009) analysis, England and Wales has significantly reduced spending on legal aid *and* courts. There hasn't, in other words, been an adjustment in the balance of assistance provided, just a marked reduction on both sides.

This is deeply suggestive of the degree to which the recent reforms have neglected to consider the legal system's needs and the structures in place to meet those needs. They have ignored, for example, the fact that more direct legal assistance and representation is needed in England and Wales than other, more inquisitorial, jurisdictions. We have an adversarial legal system governed by complex rules of argument and counter-argument in which the focus is on individual dispute. It depends, for the most part, on legal conventions and language. These are intrinsic features of our legal system; things, in other words, that the individual litigant cannot do anything to change – things that can only be changed if the system itself undergoes significant reform. We might add here that neither a shift in the balance of direct and indirect assistance, nor an overall reduction in support, is likely to serve as an instrument of ordered change.

Paterson's (2011) comparison of legal aid spending in England and Wales and Scotland illuminates this point. Scotland, Paterson points out, spends roughly a quarter less per capita on legal aid, yet the scope of the scheme is wider, both in the types of legal cases eligible for publicly funded support and the income threshold for individual eligibility. In attempting to explain how Scotland can be at once more generous in provision and spend less, Paterson argues that 'the most crucial difference between the two justice systems is that the Scots have been much more successful at holistic reform, that is, reforming court procedures (civil and criminal) to reduce legal aid spend' (Paterson, 2011: xx). In other words, here, system change has preceded and guided the balance of direct and indirect assistance. In contrast, the only notable attempt in LASPO to alter litigants' dependence on direct legal assistance involved making mediation a first-resort for divorcing couples. That this is the one system-oriented alteration in the recent reforms makes its failure all the more striking – but more on that in the following chapter.

Conclusion

In the opening decades of the 21st century, successive governments have deployed a familiar rhetoric of overspending and welfare dependency to frame legal aid as a problem. The retrenchment of legal aid – hastened by the recent reforms, but in evidence long before that – is in keeping with a broader shift in the meaning of welfare so that what was once free or subsidised for most, is now so for an ever-smaller minority. The most recent reforms have involved cuts of a different kind: a radical reduction in scope so that most areas of civil dispute are now outside of legal aid funding.

This is at odds with the original conception of legal aid as a form of social welfare available to most people, and for most legal matters. How has this shift been accomplished? It's tempting to point to the rise of austerity politics during the first decade of the 21st century and suggest that legal aid has been a victim of the allied programme of social welfare cuts. This is to see the threat to legal aid as an external one, lying principally in a changed economic-political climate. This type of argument ignores the way in which legal aid has been gradually reframed since the mid-1990s to make its retrenchment seem necessary. Take, for example, the idea that the taxpayer is a key stakeholder in legal aid reform. This has helped recast the role of the state in providing legal aid so that one of its primary responsibilities is to achieve value for money. This is by no means a discursive shift that is unique to legal aid; there has been an analogous recasting of spending on health services, with similarly drastic consequences.

This isn't to suggest, of course, that the cost of legal aid shouldn't feature at all in debates about the scheme's future. It is simply to note that the focus on cost and risk to the taxpayer has meant that arguments about the social benefit of legal aid have been sidelined. Indeed, it is a decidedly individualised view of legal aid that now predominates. The idea that the problem of legal aid is one of too many people pursuing court-based remedies contributes to this shift – again, this is an idea that was first evident in the mid-1990. This rests on the premise that the decision to litigate is purely personal and unshaped by social factors. Legal aid in turn has come to be framed as an incentive to litigate.

In debates about legal aid today the finger tends to point outwards, to the person, rather than inwards, to the distinctive needs of the system and the role of direct legal assistance within it. This obscures the fact that spending on legal aid might be higher in England and Wales – historically so, at least – but spending on courts is lower than in other, more inquisitorial, jurisdictions where court staff are able to provide greater support to litigants. We return to this point in Chapter Five. Now, we turn to review the evidence concerning the impact of the recent cuts to legal aid.

Note

[1] Scotland was exempt from this provision and still has no cap on any part of its legal aid budget.

ASSESSING THE CONSEQUENCES OF LEGAL AID REFORM IN ENGLAND AND WALES

In 2014, the National Audit Office rather damningly observed that the Ministry of Justice had implemented the far-reaching reforms introduced by the Legal Aid, Sentencing and Punishment of Offenders Act 2012 (LASPO) 'without a good understanding of why people go to court to resolve their disputes' (National Audit Office, 2014: 7, key finding 11). It highlighted a wide range of potential consequences that could stem from the cuts as unrepresented parties are left unsupported with potentially unresolved cases. It flagged the potential increased costs for the wider public sector, which may be left to pick up the pieces if an unrepresented litigant suffers mental or physical health issues due to the lack of legally funded advice and support (National Audit Office, 2014: 6, key finding 6). This chapter will consider these wide-ranging consequences, and how far alternatives such as mediation and McKenzie friends are able to plug the gap.

Thus, these far-reaching reforms have been carried out extremely quickly and apparently with little understanding of the potential impact they will have. Many organisations, including the Ministry of Justice and Legal Aid Agency (2014), the Public Accounts Committee (2015), the Low Commission (2014; 2015), and the Legal Action Group (2010) have rushed to understand the impact. Academics

(Pleasence et al, 2012; Trinder et al, 2014) and lawyers (Knight, 2014; Magistrates Association, 2015; 2016) have reported on the impact for the court, litigant and lawyer. This chapter reviews that evidence. However, as we discuss, the focus in this body of literature tends to be on measurable and tangible effects. Yet these effects, we will go on to argue in Chapter Four, are the tip of the iceberg in relation to the real impact of the reforms.

The decline in publicly funded legal advocacy and support

The cuts to legal aid have had a direct effect on the number of cases for which publicly funded legal support and representation is provided. In its review of the data, the Legal Aid Agency noted that 'acts of assistance' peaked in 2009-10 – the year before the Coalition came to power – and '[s]ince this peak the volume has fallen by just over 39 per cent; within this reduction the criminal legal aid area has reduced by almost 14 per cent but the majority of the fall has come from the civil justice area which has reduced by almost two thirds over this period' (Ministry of Justice and Legal Aid Agency, 2014: 2). Thus, civil law cases have been disproportionately affected by the cuts, with family law taking the biggest hit. In this area of practice, there was a staggering 60% drop in casework the year after LASPO came into effect (Ministry of Justice and Legal Aid Agency, 2014: 20).

Crucially, the reduction in casework has continued year on year post-LASPO. In the latest available data, from January to March 2016, civil legal aid new matter starts were down by a further 13% compared with the same period in 2015. And, despite the championing of mediation as an alternative for lawyers' involvement, numbers of mediation assessments, which fell sharply after the introduction of LASPO, were down a further 14% in the first quarter of 2016 compared with the same period in 2015. Meanwhile the number of mediation matter starts reduced by 18% over the same period (Ministry of Justice and Legal Aid Agency, 2016a: 6). The position in relation to criminal legal aid, initially protected, is now catching up, with a 9% fall in criminal workloads compared with the same period in the previous year, and a 15% reduction in spending on the scheme, mainly caused by the reduction to the fees paid for most lower tier legal aid work in crime (Ministry of Justice and Legal Aid Agency, 2016a: 6). Thus, this is a significant problem and the impact of the cuts is continuing to be felt and to deepen.

Another key issue is the apparent lack of efficacy of the safety net put into place to help litigants who are considered most in need, in the form of 'exceptional case funding' (ECF). Although provision was made to continue funding for the most vulnerable litigants, in reality this safeguard has been little used. The Legal Aid Agency planned for 5,000 to 7,000 applications in the first year post-LASPO, but only received 1,520. Of these cases, only 69 were granted funding, a tiny 5% of the expected number (Ministry of Justice and Legal Aid Agency, 2014: 7, key finding 15). This significant shortfall in the expected funding became even more pronounced in the quarter April to June 2014, with only seven cases in total being granted legal funding, so less than 1% of the predicted volume (Ministry of Justice and Legal Aid Agency, 2014). This significant shortfall resulted in the House of Commons Justice Committee concluding that, 'the exceptional cases funding scheme has not done the job Parliament intended, protecting access to justice for the most vulnerable people in our society' (2015: para 45).

However, possibly partly due to this, and also following a judicial review resulting in the application forms being simplified further, 390 applications for ECF were received between January and March 2016. This is the highest number received in a single quarter since October to December 2013. In addition, between January and March 2016, over half of those that had been determined were granted (54%) (Ministry of Justice and Legal Aid Agency, 2016a). It is too early to know whether this is a significant step in the right direction, or just a statistical blip. However, it is still much fewer than the Ministry of Justice originally expected. It equates to 1,560 cases per annum; roughly a quarter of the number it predicted.

Despite the recent upturn in ECF applications, a significant number of vulnerable litigants are still without publicly funded legal assistance.

This is significant because of the issues that can be triggered by this, such as an impact on mental or physical health, housing, or domestic violence that may be caused or exacerbated by a lack of legally funded advice and support around family law matters. These concerns have been echoed by findings both from the Low Commission (2014; 2015) and academic commentators analysing data collected by the English and Welsh Social Justice Survey (Cookson, 2011; 2013).

Both the Justice Committee (2015) and the Legal Action Group (2013) highlight how pervasive the reforms have been, and suggest that this has resulted in a widespread public perception that legal aid no longer exists. This is despite the persistent public belief that the state should fund advice on common civil legal issues, with 82% of respondents stating that such free legal advice should be available to everyone in a Legal Action Group opinion poll survey of 1,000 randomly selected members of the public (2010: 1). A similar poll carried out for London showed an even higher level of support, with 91% of respondents supporting free legal services for all (Bawdon and Hynes, 2011: 3).

Changes to the legal profession resulting from legal aid reform

The cuts to legal aid have also had a number of indirect effects. The impact on legal professionals is perhaps the most obvious of these, with the reforms prompting the closure of some solicitors' firms and a decline in the number of firms offering any publicly funded advice and assistance at all (Pleasence et al, 2012). Professional groups have greeted the new funding arrangements with great concern, with 83% of 500 senior solicitors and barristers, interviewed for research carried out by the leading law firm Hodge Jones and Allen, stating that they believed justice was no longer accessible to all (Knight, 2014: 8). In an unprecedented step, the Criminal Bar Association of England and Wales protested the new arrangements by staging a number of walkouts (BBC, 2014; Lithman, 2014). Even judges, generally known for avoiding public shows of dissent, have spoken out strongly against the cuts. Dame Elizabeth Gloster, a Court of Appeal judge, commented that she was "horrified" at the number of unrepresented litigants and warned that the delays caused will "clog up" the justice system (Bowcott, 2014).

The cuts have also put both barristers and judges in the tricky position of offering semi-formal support and advice to unrepresented litigants (Maclean and Eekelaar, 2009; Eekelaar and Maclean, 2013). New guidelines produced for lawyers by the Law Society, Chartered Institute of Legal Executives, and the Bar Council (2015a) highlight the particular tension for lawyers when they are representing one party against a litigant in person (LiP). The guidance emphasises that the duty of the lawyer to the court and the administration of justice is paramount (even above that to their own client). This leads to an uneasy tension with how much they should assist the LiP in order to fulfil that duty to the court and the effective 'administration of justice'. The guidelines state that, 'knowing and using law and procedure effectively against your opponent because you have the skills to do so, whether that be against a qualified representative or a LiP, is not taking "unfair advantage" or a breach of any regulatory code' (Law Society et al, 2015a: 5-6). And although a lawyer must not 'take unfair advantage of a LiP', they are 'under no obligation to help a LiP to run their case or to take any action on a LiP's behalf' (Law Society et al, 2015a: 6). In fact, following the case of Khudados v Hayden[1] if a lawyer does help the unrepresented opposing party, in certain circumstances they might be held to be failing in their duties to their own client.

The most significant impact of the cuts on the legal profession, though, has been the removal of a whole strand of legal professional who mainly worked on publicly funded cases, with an intrinsic emphasis on care and support for their clients. Indeed, one of the authors of this book spent the first decade of her career working in this field. Many legal aid solicitors saw their role as far closer to that of legally-enabled social worker (Eekelaar et al, 2000: 63) than to the 'city slicker' type lawyer focused on their work-in-progress and profits. A typical day could be spent drawing together a legally-coherent statement from an hour-long diatribe by a woman attempting to make ends meet when her former partner had failed to pay his maintenance payments *again*; an edge-of-the-seat hearing at the magistrates' court regarding a contact application for a father, who had previously bitten a chunk out of his ex-girlfriend's arm; and a sensitive discussion with a teenage mother facing the impossible decision of whether to agree to allow her child to be freed for adoption.

This role of 'lawyer as social worker' is one that the cuts have almost driven to extinction. In the past, this role, supported by public funding, could be seen as analogous to the NHS, a kind of 'National Legal Service'. Like the NHS, it was not without its flaws, and was undoubtedly costly to run – but it also gave a service that is unlike that offered in most other countries in the world. A service that both the public and the legal professionals are united in valuing, and united in their dismay at its ruin by such deep and arbitrary cuts. However, perhaps one of the most unsatisfactory elements is that these cuts, deep as they are, may not actually make the desired savings for the state if the knock-on consequences are taken into account. The next section and following chapter discuss the huge hidden costs caused by the 'pruning' of the legal aid lawyer, costs that are being passed on to other parts of the justice system, and beyond.

The impact of legal aid reform on the court system

One of the most widely discussed effects of the legal aid cuts has been the significant increase in LiPs, which has affected both the parties themselves and the working of the courts. Discussing the impact of the reforms, the Parliamentary Public Accounts Committee commented:

> In the year following the reforms, there was an increase of 18,519 cases (30%) in which both parties were representing themselves (known as litigants in person or LIPs) in family courts. Within this, there were 8,110 more cases involving contact with children in which both parties were LIPs in 2013-14, an increase of 89% from the previous year. Judges have estimated that cases involving LIPs can take 50% longer and many legal professionals

have said that they place additional demands upon court staff (Public Accounts Committee, 2015: para 3.16).

The Ministry of Justice and Legal Aid Agency (2014) suggest that such cases could increase the cost of financing the courts by an additional £3 million per annum (2014: key finding 6).

Perhaps unsurprisingly, the Magistrates Association gave evidence to the Committee that magistrates felt the significant rise in the number of LiPs in family courts had a negative impact on the administration of justice (Public Accounts Committee, 2015: para 3.16). LiPs frequently struggle to understand and use the complex civil law system. Court personnel, from judges to clerks, are faced with a rising number of people lost in a system that was designed for qualified lawyers, with the associated technical forms, legal jargon and formality. Those assessing the impact of legal aid reform have particularly emphasised this set of problems – and we turn to this body of literature in due course (Trinder et al, 2014; Magistrates Association, 2015; Public Accounts Committee, 2015). For now we want to point out that this focus is perhaps at the expense of research on the impact for litigants before even reaching court. Previously, not only would eligible parties have publicly funded representation from their solicitor in court, but they would also, and perhaps most valuably, receive support and advice before court proceedings. In fact, this support and advice, and the negotiations between two separate family law solicitors on behalf of the parties, would often negate the need for court proceedings. Thus, cases would be diverted from the courts, litigation (costly in time, money and emotions) could be avoided, and a solution that was (ideally) better suited for both parties would be reached, with a level of agreement and compromise. The decline of this form of support helps explain why, contrary to the government's stated aim of reducing the number of contested family cases that reached the courts, there was an *increase* in the number of such cases reaching the courts post-LASPO, with the figure rising from 64% in 2012-13 to 89% in 2013-14 (National Audit Office, 2014).

The impact of legal aid reform on litigants

Current research on litigants without lawyers is sparse, as Trinder et al (2014) note in a study commissioned by the Ministry of Justice. This research was carried out by a consortium of academics from six universities and included observations of 151 private law family cases where a hearing was observed, the court file examined, and parties and professionals interviewed. To provide wider context, focus groups were also held with judges, court staff and lawyers. The research resulted in a 234-page report on the state of private family law cases for LiPs in a post-LASPO context. It comments, 'Follow up independent research is needed to examine the impact of legal aid reforms on the types and experiences of LiPs, their impact on the court system and the effectiveness of innovations and services to support LiPs' (Trinder et al, 2014: 8). This is largely because much of the research that does exist (with the notable exception of Maclean and Eekelaar, 2016) focuses on measurable outcomes, notably: duration of process, impact on court staff, and trial outcomes (Ministry of Justice and Legal Aid Agency, 2014a; Magistrates Association, 2015). This is perhaps unsurprising as these are the more tangible effects that concern the Ministry of Justice. However, there are intrinsic problems with these measurable outcomes, even if they are deemed to signal 'success'. Duration is a case in point: a quick outcome does not necessarily equate to a 'good' outcome as one of the parties may restart the legal process due to a lack of legal representation, or feeling railroaded into a decision by the speed of the process. The report by Trinder et al (2014), as well as outlining the impact from a more systems-based perspective when parties were unrepresented, does make an effective attempt at considering the perceptions and experiences of LiPs, and identifying some of the key problems they experienced.

The report identifies four different types of unrepresented party in family proceedings. First, the proactive, capable and organised litigant; secondly, and in contrast, the proactive but disorganised litigant. Thirdly, the reactive litigant who may respond to suggestions by the judge or other legal professionals, especially if such instructions are clear and precise, but was unable to take an initiative or successfully run their own case unaided. Forthly, the passive or chaotic litigant, who either relied on others to provide help and initiative, or who did not even engage with the court at all, due to hostility or because of a chaotic lifestyle. However, one uniting factor the report concluded ran through most of the parties acting for themselves post-LASPO was that mainly people were conducting family cases themselves due to the lack of affordability of legal representation, rather than due to a free-will choice. Many also reported significant frustration at the lack of free or low-cost legal advice in the community, with LiPs reporting that even Citizen Advice Bureaux (CAB) were not able to offer true 'legal' advice, and – perhaps more understandably – neither would Cafcass[2] or the courts. This caused a number of problems for both the parties and the court system. The report found that even people who were highly educated or had professional experience frequently could not represent themselves competently within the unfamiliar, jargon-heavy environment of the court. They were frequently faced with attempting to handle complex cases, which, because of their nature involving issues surrounding children, the family home and livelihoods, were highly emotionally charged. LiPs had limited understanding of disclosure rules, or the expectation placed on litigants to negotiate and attempt to reach a settlement.

To compound these problems, the report found that there had been limited adaptation of the current system – and especially forms – for LiPs, leaving them faced with legalese and lengthy documentation, numerous deadlines and filing requirements that were both unfamiliar and demanding. Trinder et al (2014) recommend the creation of a dedicated website for LiPs where accessible information and all the required forms are gathered together. The Judicial Working Group on Litigants in Person (2013) has also called for the Ministry of Justice and the courts to devote resources to producing audiovisual material to inform LiPs about what they can expect when they go to court, and what is required of them. It also recommended that a thorough review of web-based information was urgently undertaken, to ensure LiPs could easily access the information, understand the process and decide on the best course of action to prepare and present their case (The Judicial Working Group on Litigants in Person, 2013: 32). Videos and online material for LiPs is now available, including guidance and some downloadable forms (Ministry of Justice, 2016b). However, the then Chief Executive of HM Courts and Tribunals Service, Natalie Ceeney, when giving evidence to the House of Commons Justice Committee, stated that the wording of forms still needs to be improved to help LiPs. Now four years after the reforms were brought in, LiPs are still faced with completing the same forms that were designed for trained lawyers to complete and understand. Ceeney commented:

> so many forms are written in legalese and you need a legal degree to be able to fill them out…One of the challenges is to turn the forms in plain English. We have created the problem for ourselves by making the system so hard to use (in Hyde, 2015).

The impact of legal aid reform on the work of the court

Trinder et al (2014) found that LiPs struggled to navigate the complex civil law system. Conversely, from the perspective of the courts, LiPs could be seen as presenting some problems for the smooth-running of the court system (Magistrates Association, 2015). Hearings where the parties were legally represented were described as 'patterned, predictable and efficient' (Trinder et al, 2014: 4). Whereas the report described circumstances at hearings with unrepresented parties as presenting a range of problems including complete non-appearance, refusal to engage with the hearing, and less frequently, violent or aggressive behaviour. In more cases, the unrepresented party required significant guidance and time from the court staff on the process. Trinder et al (2014) note that this presents particular difficulties given that court staff may be unwilling or unable to give such support due to time constraints or lack of knowledge. And, even when staff do have the time and knowledge available, there is a tension between giving basic advice and giving legal advice. Where is the line drawn between explaining what is required and what a form is asking, and giving (legal) advice about the appropriate way to complete it?

The increase of unrepresented parties also impacts on the conduct of hearings themselves. The report (Trinder et al, 2014) categorised hearings with unrepresented parties as either relatively fair and efficient, or generally unfair and/or inefficient. It then usefully subdivided each into four categories, highlighting the key factors that affected such outcomes. The 'fair/efficient' hearings were characterised as 'Umbrella' hearings, which occurred if only one side was represented and the lawyer ended up working for both sides to some extent to ensure the smooth running of the process. Alternatively, if neither side was represented, then a third party sometimes acted as a 'quasi' lawyer, or, in the case of child contact cases, the children's appointed lawyer acted as a broker for both LiPs. Thirdly, in some 'fair and efficient' cases the family judge took an active role, in a similar way as the continental inquisitorial system. Finally, a competent 'holding-their-own' LiP may be able to manage a simple hearing entirely unrepresented, with some support from the judge. Trinder et al (2014) suggest that the impact of the legal aid cuts is most evident in hearings that are characterised as 'generally inefficient/unfair'. The report highlighted 'Hot Potato' chaotic interim hearings with disruptive LiPs as particularly problematic, not least because they frequently resulted in fully contested hearings. Three particular types of LiP were highlighted as especially likely to be involved in 'Hot Potato' hearings. First, the over-confident LiP whose interventions led to rambling hearings. Secondly, the out-of-their-depth LiP who neither understood the process, nor was able to accomplish any tasks required, resulting in long and/or additional hearings before any outcome could be achieved. Finally, the unprotected LiP, who was unable to present their case properly or explain and explore their concerns.

The report (Trinder et al, 2014) emphasises the significant need for support for unrepresented parties given the problems already outlined. It highlights the positive impact of either the judge or the solicitor for the other party taking time to explain things to an unrepresented litigant. However, as already discussed, this does have significant impact for the lawyer in both time and potential blurring of roles and responsibilities. From the perspective of the litigant, more positive outcomes were achieved by those that had previous experiences of being at court, and a level of confidence that enabled them to be proactive in the process, but not too much so that they were unwilling to take any advice or guidance from the court officials or other lawyers. The report sets out a whole raft of practical, emotional and procedural issues that could be addressed to help unrepresented parties, and enable the family court system to continue to operate, despite currently groaning under the pressure of an increasing number of LiPs.

Trinder et al (2014) also put forward a number of procedural changes to accommodate the rise in LiPs in the civil law courts. They suggest that courts should be responsible for giving more information to LiPs before the first hearing and suggest that judges should be encouraged to give clearer guidance and verbal instruction during those hearings. There should also be more opportunity for face-to-face enquiries provided by court staff. The report also recognised the significant emotional burden of family court proceedings on litigants, and the need for greater emotional support. This could include streamlining the procedure to allow family members to attend the court hearing to support the litigant (currently they must submit a formal CV to court to gain permission to attend the family hearing). Incorporating and regulating non-legal support services was also highlighted. Interestingly, to some extent this has been addressed by judges by their welcoming of schemes such as CLOCK, set up by the University of Keele, and now spread across many university law schools countrywide, to give support (but not legal advice) to litigants in the family courts (CLOCK, 2016). This scheme is discussed in greater depth later in the chapter.

On a practical level, the report called for initial legal advice to be made universally available to facilitate dispute resolution and called for the judiciary to accept a major shift in their role to see a key part of it as now being to support LiPs. It highlighted the need for there to be greater accessibility for ECF, which has been significantly underused. As a way of facilitating this, it proposes a mechanism for judges to recommend funded representation in the interests of justice, which could be an ideal step forward – especially if this could bypass litigants applying themselves. It is frequently the litigant who is least able to complete the forms or understand the process who is most in need of the help and support that funded legal advice would provide.

Trinder et al's (2014) report is not the only one to highlight how the rise of LiP has affected the work of the court. Of particular note is work carried out by the Magistrates Association, which conducted two surveys of members on the impact of LiPs in the magistrates' courts, in February and November 2014. About private law family matters, magistrates were asked their opinion of whether the increasing numbers of unrepresented parties had an adverse impact on the courts. Over 50% of magistrates stated that it had an adverse impact 'most' or 'all' of the time (62% in the first survey and 58% in the second), with a further third stating that it 'occasionally' had an adverse impact (34% and 37% respectively). None responded that it 'never' had any adverse impact (Magistrates Association, 2015: 3). In addition, the survey showed that the numbers of parties representing themselves rose from 46% in the first survey to 60% in the second (Magistrates Association, 2015: 7).

A lacuna of legal advice and support

Considerable attention has been given to the impact of LASPO on litigation and the courtroom. The effect of the reforms on civil legal advice and assistance has received less scrutiny. Yet this is where the cuts have been deepest, as mentioned in Chapter One. The notable exception here is the Low Commission (2014; 2015), a group of independent commissioners set up to study the impact of LASPO on legal advice concerning social welfare law. Their work has been mainly directed towards tracing the impact of legal aid reform on advisory services, and to this end they carried out research on five different regions: Tameside, Swansea and Neath Port Talbot, Gloucestershire, Bristol, and Kensington and Chelsea (Low Commission, 2014: 9-10).

The Commission's reports highlight an 'advice deficit' post-LASPO that has been significantly worsened by cuts to local government services (Low Commission, 2015: 19). They point out that the wider political and economic context – specifically the cuts to social welfare services – mean that this deficit comes at a time of increased need (Low Commission, 2014: 1). This is their point of departure for assessing legal advisory services post-LASPO. Their research reveals a wholesale transformation in provision:

> Twenty years ago over 10,000 solicitors' offices offered publicly funded legal advice through the civil legal aid (green form) scheme across most areas of law, working alongside a Citizens Advice network that ran 721 CABx operating from multiple access points, and a growing Law Centres movement. Today less than 2,000 firms offer any civil legal aid at all with many fewer firms than that providing social welfare advice...only 21 [CABx] offer specialist civil legal aid advice compared to over 200 just five years ago...[I]t is impossible to come to any other conclusion that key services are being eroded over time (Low Commission, 2015: 20).

The erosion of key advisory services has in turn meant that front-line staff are increasingly struggling to point people towards appropriate services. The CAB undertook a survey of its bureaux in 2014, and found that '92% of them now struggle to find anywhere to refer people, with complex cases whom they cannot help, on to other organisations that would be able to help them' (Low Commission, 2015: 49). People are turning elsewhere for legal advice, and often to organisations that lack the specialist training and resources to cater to this additional work, such as MPs (Low Commission, 2014: 11).

Alternative sources of support for litigants

We turn here to consider two key areas of support that have grown up to support LiPs post-LASPO: firstly volunteer helpers akin to McKenzie friends giving support at the county courts and secondly, mediation mainly by professionally trained mediators.

The rise and diversification of McKenzie friends

The term 'McKenzie friend' derives from *McKenzie v McKenzie* [1971] P 33, a decision by the Court of Appeal.[3] Levine McKenzie, a petitioner in divorce proceedings, lodged an appeal on the basis that the trial judge had denied him the opportunity to receive limited assistance from an Australian barrister, Ian Hangar, who was not qualified to practice in the UK. The judge ruled that Mr Hangar must sit in the public gallery during the hearing, and that he could only advise Mr McKenzie during adjournments. The Court of Appeal subsequently ruled that the trial judge's decision had denied Mr McKenzie rightful assistance, in the form of taking notes, and quietly making suggestions and advice as the hearing proceeded.

Post-LASPO, the McKenzie friend has become an increasingly common courtroom participant though, again, there isn't solid data concerning the use of this support. Nonetheless, legal and judicial groups have noted the increased uptake and in turn recognise the need to reform the role. In 2016, the Judicial Office published a consultation paper on reforming the courts' approach to McKenzie friends (Judicial Office, 2016) in which they asked whether the term should be replaced by a 'more readily understandable' term, and whether a new code of conduct should govern the role. The Magistrates Association (2016) agreed that the term was technical and not readily understandable by all LiPs, and that a new term such as 'Court User Supporter' would be preferable (Magistrates Association, 2016: 1).

This shift in nomenclature would certainly help in capturing the rise of informal 'soft legal' in-court support that has emerged post-LASPO. The Personal Support Unit (2012) trains volunteers who give such assistance in both courts and tribunals in London and 13 other cities around the country. Another notable, and as yet under-researched, phenomenon is the growth of student volunteers acting as helpers in this way, mainly from local university law schools. There has been an established tradition of university law schools offering pro bono legal advice at Law Centres, with students offering advice overseen by legally qualified solicitors (for examples, see Nottingham Trent

University, 2016; University of Manchester, 2016). However, the CLOCK (2016) scheme – initiated by the University of Keele in 2012 and now made up of a consortium of universities across the country – has a different approach. The scheme aims to offer help and support to unrepresented parties in the county courts – but expressly does not give legal advice. This perhaps highlights the key role that family law solicitors played, over and above purely being purveyors of legal advice, in the amount of both emotional and practical support that they were giving to their clients. The student volunteers, known as Community Legal Companions, are drawn from law students, receive five day's training before starting on the programme, and commit to giving two hours per week to assist unrepresented parties attending the county court for hearings. This assistance includes completing court forms, arranging court papers, taking notes and accompanying LiPs into court (under McKenzie friend principles). They also signpost to legal aid solicitors, charitable organisations, fixed fee legal service providers, and mediators. Some University of Brighton students who had acted as Community Legal Companions and were asked to reflect on the process and the assistance they offered commented, "[LiPs are] lost in the system"…"We are a bridge, someone to talk to, they can't talk to Court staff"…"We can make it simpler for people" (Ashton, 2016).

The Judicial Working Group on Litigants in Person (2013), which was formed at the request of the Master of the Rolls, produced a report on the impact of LASPO for LiPs that echoes the sentiments of these students' comments. It stressed that litigants should not be viewed as 'a problem' but that 'the problem lies with a system which has not developed with a focus on unrepresented litigants' (Judicial Working Group, 2013: 6). The report also highlights the increasing role that McKenzie friends would be likely to take in the process, and the nuanced response that was required for this given the variety and differing motivations of people involved. The report points out that whereas some people acting as a McKenzie friend behave helpfully by taking notes or giving quiet suggestions and support as the hearing proceeded, they were concerned about the proliferation of 'professional' McKenzie friends. These lay advocates were of concern because they sought to assist an unrepresented party for a fee, but without the requisite training or regulation of a professional lawyer. They commented, 'some of these representatives charge fees, which are similar if not more than those of a professional lawyer. Some are unable effectively to represent the litigant. Some are positively disruptive to the proceedings' (Judicial Working Group, 2013: 27).

The Magistrates Association (2016) notes a similar problem in their research. A survey of their members highlighted that McKenzie friends on occasion cause disruption when they attempt to go beyond their role, particularly to the right of audience.[4] The Magistrates Association nonetheless concluded by stating:

> LiPs have a right to reasonable assistance and that may be provided by family or friends. The MA [Magistrates Association] would be very concerned if genuine attempt to regulate McKenzie Friends such as signing a code of conduct or filling out a form put off friends or family who were just there for moral support (Magistrates Association, 2016: 4).

This points to the need for greater checks and balances in relation to the distinctive support offered by McKenzie friends, and the complexities of regulating this form of legal support.

The role of mediation post-LASPO

The development of the practice of mediation (initially known as conciliation) can be traced back to its endorsement by the Finer Committee on One-Parent families in the 1970s (Manchester and Whetton, 1974; Dingwall and Eekelaar, 1988). It first gained public funding in 1996 via the Legal Aid Board, with the introduction of a Code of Practice and a competency test (Roberts, 2005). Over the years, this has been overseen by a number of bodies, initially the College of Family Mediators, which was superseded by the Family Mediation Council. This in turn had a number of member organisations, including the Law Society, Resolution, and the

Alternative Dispute Resolution Group. Thus, there was a significant divergence in the ways mediation developed, and the ethos behind each: many mediators also being trained lawyers, but others not.

It is difficult to assess how many mediation sessions are carried out in total, as ones that are not publicly funded may not be recorded. However, of publicly funded mediation between 2006/7 and 2013/4, there was an average of 13,378 mediations a year. This masks a significant fall from 15,357 sessions in 2011/2 to 8,432 sessions in 2013/4 (Ministry of Justice and Legal Aid Agency, 2014: 55, Table 7.2). This reduction may become even greater as 31% of legal aid firms indicated in 2012 that they may not still be carrying out legal aid work in three years' time, including legally-funded mediation (Pleasence et al, 2012: ii). This will potentially leave the LiP with even less support as even the avenue of mediation may become unavailable for many with further reductions in legal aid suppliers. We come back to consider these matters in Chapter Four.

The point to stress here is that one of the key aims of the government when introducing LASPO was to promote the use of mediation as a way to reduce public funding costs and attempt to prevent cases reaching the courts. Traditionally, or at least in the eyes of the government, lawyers were associated with litigation, mediators with reconciliation. However, many mediators are also legally qualified, and many lawyers also act as mediators. This is by no means to suggest that one can replace the other. In fact, when 'information meetings' were introduced under the Family Law Act 1996 as a form of mediation that had to be undertaken before issuing divorce proceedings, research found that they did little to entice parties away from lawyers in favour of mediation (Eekelaar et al, 2000: 1-9). This is perhaps because parties valued the importance of the support and individual advice that they received from their lawyer. We discuss this issue in greater depth in Chapter Four. Here, we'll simply observe that the information meetings introduced in the mid-1990s were quickly abandoned. However, the requirement in the Family Law Act 1996 that a party who was seeking legal funding must first attend a mediation meeting (unless particular exceptions were met), remained in the Legal Services Commission Funding Code.[5] This was perhaps the thin end of the wedge towards cutting publicly funded advice and assistance. This promotion of mediation continued under LASPO as a primary service for separating couples in place of legal assistance, the assumption being that the retrenchment of civil legal aid would force an increase in take-up.

Conclusion

This chapter has considered the impact of the LASPO reforms, the research, and the public and legal outcry and media comment that has stemmed from this. As we started the chapter, we will end by considering the National Audit Office observation that 'the Ministry implemented the reforms without a good understanding of why people go to court to resolve their disputes' (National Audit Office, 2014: 7, key finding 11). This chapter serves to show the grave difficulties that this lack of research and understanding at the outset has caused.

Policy and research largely neglects the impact on LiPs *before* the court process, focusing instead on statistics and measurable outcomes in relation to the court process, the effects on court staff, and trial outcomes. There are exceptions to this – notably Maclean and Eekelaar (2016) and the Low Commission (2014; 2015) – but the focus here tends to be on providing advisory services, rather than the role and function of legal assistance. Thus, the service that was previously the mainstay of legal aid lawyers' work has been largely neglected: that is, the giving of support and advice to clients in the solicitor's office – not at the court. The direct effect of LASPO on legal advice and litigants is the issue we will return to in the next chapter. This is the area where the uncomfortable juxtaposition of the government's focus on statistics, economics and savings is brought into sharpest focus against the lived reality of the impact of the cuts for individuals. People who are attempting to act for themselves in the family courts, and dealing with the emotional and personal issues of resolving arrangements about children and the family home, potentially against a backdrop of at worst domestic violence, or at least feelings of resentment and antagonism towards (or from) their former partner or spouse. Current research only addresses the tip of the iceberg when considering the far-reaching impact of these cuts.

Notes

1   Khudados v Hayden [2007] EWCA Civ 1316 para 38.
2   Child and Family Court Advisory and Support Service.
3   (1970) 3 W.L.R. 472; (1970) 3 All E.R. 1034; (1970) 114 S.J. 667.
4   The 'right of audience' is a common law right of a lawyer to appear and conduct proceedings in court on behalf of their client. In superior courts, generally only barristers or advocates have a right of audience (unless a solicitor has obtained a Certificate of Advocacy). Solicitors generally have a right of audience in the magistrates, county and district courts (for the jurisdiction that they have qualified). A LiP also has a right of audience but, crucially, a person who is not a qualified lawyer does not have a right of audience in court to represent someone else.
5   LSC Funding Code 3C-454: 'the client must attend a meeting with a mediator or otherwise satisfy the requirement under Criterion 11.12.2 before funding by way of Family Help (Higher) Legal Representation will be granted'.

4

TOWARDS A HOLISTIC CONCEPTION OF LEGAL AID

The previous chapter examined the evidence on the impact of the recent reforms to legal aid. We argued there that policy debate and research has focused almost entirely on the decline of publicly funded legal representation and its impact on courtroom proceedings. The cuts to civil legal advice and assistance have received very little attention, with the notable exception of the Low Commission's (2014; 2015) recent reports on social welfare law. This gap is particularly surprising given that, on closer inspection, it is pre-litigation support that has been most affected by the cuts. The most recent statistics released by the Ministry of Justice and Legal Aid Agency (2016a) reveal that funding for civil legal help is at two thirds of its pre- Legal Aid, Sentencing and Punishment of Offenders Act 2012 (LASPO) level, while funding for civil legal representation has declined by a more modest third. Thus, in this chapter we argue that a more holistic conception of legal aid is needed, one that takes account of the role of legal help and the experiences of litigants. This, in turn, will allow us to arrive at a better understanding of the impact of recent reform.

To this end, the first half of this chapter examines the role of the solicitor in giving advice and assistance, with a particular emphasis on the family lawyer, although many of these issues may in fact equally apply to legal aid lawyers more broadly. We compare the solicitor's role with that of the mediator – not, to be clear, to suggest that this form of support is inherently better or worse, but rather to give a clearer sense of what has been lost with the cuts to legal help. Without legal advice, disputants are liable to be left feeling deeply frustrated and overwhelmed. The absence of this advice risks transforming the law into nothing more than a brute edifice, comprehensible to those with power and status, and utterly unassailable to those without. Thus, in assessing the value of legal advice, this chapter suggests the importance of a litigant-focused perspective.

The role and value of legal advice and assistance

In Chapter Two we noted that there was a shift during the mid-1980s in the way legal aid came to be discussed, both in public debate and policy documents. It was during this time that legal aid first came to be seen as a problem of overspending and lack of government control. Lawyers were seen as central to this problem, the presumption being that they had a vested interest in pushing up the cost of legal aid provision. In the 21st century this view of lawyers has become dominant, to such a degree that policy documents tend to presume that the work lawyers do in providing advice is principally directed towards transforming disputants into litigants. In the 2010 green paper on legal aid reform, for example, the work lawyers do is consistently elided with litigation and their work understood narrowly, in terms of 'specific professional expertise' (Ministry of Justice, 2010: 35). Yet there is a rich body of academic literature that suggests legal advice involves much more than this (Ingleby, 1992; Davis et al, 1994; Eekelaar et al, 2000; Hitchings et al, 2013).

Legal advice, and the negotiations between two separate solicitors on behalf of the parties, often negates the need for court proceedings at all. Contrary to government assertion (and perhaps common perception) that lawyers tend to increase animosity and the likelihood of litigation between parties, empirical research shows that in most cases the opposite is the case. Solicitors tend to take an instrumental and proactive role in solving problems (Lewis, 2000), and are often reluctant to litigate if a fair settlement could be reached for their client without resorting to the courts (Davis et al, 1994; Ingleby, 1992). In fact, in stark contrast to the official line on litigation and dispute, a *very small* proportion of justiciable problems end up in court – just 5%, in the last round of the Civil and Social Justice Panel Survey (CSJPS), conducted in 2010 (Pleasence et al, 2011: 50).

There is considerable evidence that solicitors are especially important in resolving disputes before they get to court. In a study looking at how and why divorcing couples reach financial settlement, Hitchings et al (2013: 36-7) found that most (60%) uncontested financial consent orders in their sample were obtained in solicitor-led disputes. What's more, survey data from the CSJPS indicate that the vast majority of people value lawyers' support and advice. Based on a sample of 3,806 adults, the last wave of the survey in 2010 showed that nearly 90% of people are satisfied with solicitors' advice on civil law matters. In fact, just over a third (34%) reported being 'extremely satisfied' with this input (Pleasence et al, 2011: 47). And the CSJPS shows up the diffuse effect of legal advice: 44% of respondents noted that this form of support led to improvements in other areas of their lives, such as health and overall wellbeing (Pleasence et al, 2011: 49). All this begs the question: what exactly do solicitors do to help people settle their disputes?

Settling a dispute takes time and, in many cases, considerable effort. Research on the process of dispute-resolution for divorcing couples indicates that emotional readiness is a key factor (Hitchings et al, 2013). Time and distance help achieve this; legal advice plays a role too by enabling arm's length negotiation and clarity about each party's legal rights and responsibilities. It's worth noting that a significant proportion of people entering into a dispute have no or limited knowledge of their legal rights. In the 2010 round of the CSJPS just over a third of respondents reported having no legal knowledge at the outset of their dispute, with a further fifth reporting that they only had a partial understanding (Pleasence et al, 2011: ii). The law is of course not the only means of resolving a dispute, but in the case of highly emotionally-charged disputes between ex-couples where each party might be suspicious of the other's ability to act fairly, it can provide an important benchmark.

In practical terms, this may require a solicitor giving firm advice to her client that their position is untenable, that they will not win at court, and that they should not pursue their case in the way they propose. A particular example of this is the aggrieved husband who feels that as he paid the lion's share of the mortgage while the wife mainly looked after the children, he should be able to keep the house, and the wife should be the one to move out. Alternatively, a parent paying maintenance to the Child Maintenance Service (formerly Child Support Agency) may feel they have a right to contact with their children as they are 'paying'. A family law solicitor would have previously dealt with these issues, giving – and potentially repeating several times – advice on the realities of the law. This may take the form of advice setting out the requirements enshrined in statute that the welfare of the child should be of paramount concern, and that housing that child until they reached majority, would be one of the court's key aims. And this, a family solicitor would point out, comes above and beyond financial considerations, for example, who has previously paid the mortgage.

Formerly, this was the bread-and-butter work solicitors did in providing legal advice. In fact, it is reasonable to suggest that legal aid solicitors historically had a particularly key role in negotiation and problem-solving. As Genn and Beinart (1999), in their groundbreaking study of pathways to justice, observe, 'those who seek [publicly funded legal] advice ostensibly about a single issue may have a bundle of underlying problems or difficulties that require unpacking before any viable resolution can be achieved' (Genn and Beinart, 1999: 36). Thus, in discussing the role of the legal aid lawyer, Eekelaar et al describe it as 'a mixture of a general medical practitioner and a social worker with clout' (Eekelaar et al, 2000: 63). The role involves a high level of interactivity and support, and an ability to both ascertain the client's wishes, and then negotiate effectively for these. This enables the client to find a path through the technicalities of the legal system to reach an outcome that satisfies their needs, and ideally those of the other party.

It's worth pausing here to note an important difference between the publicly funded family lawyer and the family lawyer paid directly by their client. Maclean and Eekelaar (2016) argue that the former takes the client's instructions and negotiates a strategy with them, but is mindful of duties to court and legal aid authorities. In contrast, the privately paid family lawyer 'looks more like the adversarial commercially minded stereotypes of the divorce lawyer, largely because he accepts his client's instructions rather than negotiating a strategy with him' (Eekelaar et al, 2000: 79). Many privately paid family lawyers may protest that this is indeed a stereotype – especially as many are also now trained mediators – but would nevertheless accept that who is 'paying the piper' does cause a shift in the relationship between solicitor and client. With this, there may be less need to problem-solve and mediate, rather than litigate. All of this is to suggest that the legal aid lawyer provides a distinctive form of advocacy. This should make us think again about how the cuts to legal aid are affecting the legal profession. It's not simply a matter of the number of lawyers being reduced, but a very particular type of legal advocacy being eroded: one which has customarily needed to take a holistic view of the disputant and her problems.

Mediation as a form of dispute resolution

Thinking about the solicitor's role in giving advice and support should give us pause to reconsider the failure of mediation to become a remedy of first resort. This is partly, as discussed in Chapter Three, due to the removal of legal help to signpost this service. It is also possibly linked to mediators' different style of practice as compared with that of the lawyer (notwithstanding that a mediator may also be a trained lawyer). Family mediators deal with a discrete set of issues connected with relationship breakdown and work for both parties equally and impartially (Parkinson, 2014). They may give *information* about the legal process, but should not give legal *advice* on outcome or likelihood of success for one or the other party – we return to this distinction in due course. In addition, mediators tend to work more frequently in the context of face-to-face mediation meetings, with little contact with the parties outside these meetings. They also have fewer infrastructures to support them, and are less likely to have a secretary or assistant who could take messages or deal with queries when they are in other mediation sessions or away from the office. Therefore, outside the context of that meeting, litigants may feel very much alone and – crucially – are still faced with conducting their legal case unrepresented if a settlement cannot be reached.

Another key issue, and one that affects not only mediators, but all other services that support litigants without giving legal advice (such as McKenzie friends, court staff, and CAB workers), is the thorny question of what is 'information' and what is 'advice'. The Family Mediation Council Code of Practice and Guidance states that mediators must remain impartial. They 'may inform participants of possible courses of action, their legal or other implications, and assist them to explore these, *but must make it clear that they are not giving advice'* [italics added] (Family Mediation Council, 2016: section 5.3). However, MacLean and Eekelaar (2016: 84-5) question whether a distinction between advice and information is realistic, arguing that it must be impossible to conduct a meaningful mediation session without giving advice on process, even if not on outcome. They also point out that what is defined as information and advice can vary depending on context: "I wouldn't go into that field, if I were you, it is full of poisonous snakes," could be construed as advice, whereas a notice on the perimeter fence informing the public at large that the field contains poisonous snakes would merely be general information. Roberts agrees that the distinction is 'more complex than it sounds' (2014: 11), and can cause particular difficulties for the legally-trained mediator, who may feel exasperated that a mediation is stalling if they know that it is because one of the parties is taking a position that would not stand up in law. She quotes one mediator as saying:

> That was one situation where I actually thought the legal situation was important. So I said: "Look the legal position is this. It is no good waving your papers and saying you are going

to law because there is nothing for you to gain. So can we put all that to one side and get on with the actual issues that we can agree or disagree about" (Roberts, 2007: 136).

This demonstrates the difficulty for a mediator in treading the line between facilitating the process and giving advice. It also shows the potential difficulty faced by a litigant in person (LiP) in such a situation, who is likely to feel undermined and confused by being told they are wrong in law by someone who is meant to be impartial and assisting both sides. To sum up, the distinction between information and advice 'will not always be easy to sustain, and disputing parties might be forgiven for mistaking the former...for the latter' (Boulle and Nesic, 2001: 172-73).

In fact, as Hitchings and Miles (2016) point out, mediators in England and Wales have historically worked in a complementary fashion to solicitors in guiding divorcing couples towards a resolution. Divorcing couples value expert legal knowledge about what a court would be likely to award, even if they are undertaking mediation, to gain a sense of fairness and balance. The idea is that the 'mediator takes an impartial approach towards facilitating settlement' while each party receives 'tailored, partisan legal advice' that provides them with 'some understanding of the potential (and limits) of their legal rights and obligations' (Hitchings and Miles, 2016: 175). They point out that, without the latter:

> the autonomy apparently exercised in mediation devolves into a somewhat limited, formal autonomy only, and the supposed freedom of choice being exercised somewhat empty. Settlement for settlement's sake may be more dangerous than no settlement at all (Hitchings and Miles, 2016: 176).

They draw attention to the problems faced by mediators when one or both parties are without legal support, a situation that LASPO has made significantly more common. For one thing, mediators now often find themselves under pressure to provide legal advice and settle

LEGAL AID IN CRISIS

what remains, in essence, a legal dispute. The knock-on effect is that mediation may become more directive and, in turn, less oriented towards therapeutic goals (Hitchings and Miles, 2016: 191). In other words, it risks becoming neither one thing nor the other.

Bridging the justice gap

To see mediation as a substitute for legal advice is, then, to ignore the distinctive value of each. Why haven't these differences in provision received greater attention in policy debates? One explanation is that the government has adopted the rhetoric that family law disputes are essentially private concerns and, in turn, dispute resolution is a simple matter of getting the parties to talk things through and reach a mutually-beneficial solution. Thus, the official view is that a good number of legal disputes, particularly those related to family law:

> result from a litigant's *own decisions* in their *personal life*. Where the issue is one which arises from the litigant's *own personal choices*, we are not likely to consider that these cases concern issues of the highest importance (Ministry of Justice, 2010: para 4.19 – italics added).

What such a view ignores – indeed, flatly denies (note the repetition of 'own' and 'personal') – is that the stakes involved in family law cases generally go beyond pursuing 'personal choice'. In fact, the stakes are often exceptionally high, involving contact with children, long-term financial security, and on occasion the ability to leave an abusive relationship. The language of personal decision-making also obscures the degree to which legal disputes – family law cases in particular – are underwritten by stark, socially-produced differences in power. After all, the family is still based on an unequal division of labour, where women normally juggle work and childcare while men work full time. When couples separate, the resulting dispute is frequently shaped by inequalities of income and family responsibility. Think, for a moment, about the stay-at-home mother in dispute with an ex-partner about child contact arrangements, the part-time female worker trying to settle a divorce with a better-off spouse, and the lone mother separating from an abusive ex-husband. To see these disputes as a matter of personal choice is to neglect the ways in which they arise from and are shaped by social arrangements.

In short, disputes are irrevocably social, frequently involve the exercise of power, and exacerbate inequalities. The neglect of these simple but crucial ideas has allowed for a widening of the gap between those who are able to push for an outcome in their favour and those who lack the means to do so. The cuts to legal advice and assistance for civil disputes are part of a bigger picture. Take, for example, the introduction of court fees on the basis (again) that many disputes are private matters that should be paid for by the litigant, rather than the taxpayer. Within this, there is a move towards raising court charges so that they exceed the cost of providing a service – so-called 'enhanced fees' (Secondary Legislation Scrutiny Committee HL, 2015). The most recent report by the European Commission for the Efficiency of Justice (2016) gives some insight into the impact of this development. It points to a 37% increase in the annual income received from court charges in England and Wales between 2012 and 2014 (2016: 64). Again, as with the cuts to legal aid, private family law matters have been particularly affected by the increases in court charges. The Civil Proceedings, Family Proceedings, and Upper Tribunal Fees (Amendment) Order 2016 raised the fee for an uncontested divorce by 35% to £550. The Ministry of Justice estimates that the cost of processing an uncontested divorce is £270 (Secondary Legislation Scrutiny Committee HL, 2015). That's a profit of £280, just over 100% of the cost of administration.

The stated rationale for 'enhanced fees' might be to increase the financial viability of the justice system as a whole, but it's difficult not to see this hike in court charges as a means of punishing people for 'choosing' to get divorced. Indeed, in discussing this fee increase, the House of Lords Secondary Legislation Committee (2015) raised precisely this concern. Moreover, to ignore the possibility that this increase in costs may contribute to the parties' unequal footing is to refuse the social factors involved in family law disputes, and particularly the role of gender. Women are nearly twice as likely to apply for a divorce than men (Secondary Legislation Scrutiny Committee HL, 2015: Point 7). This observation should give us pause to recognise (again) that family law disputes are often products of social arrangements, rather than straightforward choice. Current arrangements in the legal system not only deny that possibility; they work to deepen the underlying inequalities that inform disputes.

Moreover, they risk producing a profound sense of injustice among litigants, around the outcome of their dispute as well as the legal system more broadly. Without publicly funded legal advice, litigants involved in family law cases are faced with 'going it alone'. The first part of this chapter discussed in some detail the role of legal advice in resolving disputes. We want to emphasise a key issue implicit to our discussion: the lack of legal advice means that litigants have little opportunity to work through the gap between how they think a dispute should be resolved, and how a dispute is conceived of in legal terms. Of fundamental importance to solicitors' task of getting clients emotionally ready to settle a dispute is equipping them with the means of *reconciling* their sense of justice with that enshrined in law. That gap is in some cases unbridgeable, and in others negotiated with a good deal of ambivalence. In general, though, it's reasonable to suggest that the greater understanding disputants have of the legal basis for resolving a dispute, the quicker they will reach agreement and the more likely they are to feel that justice has been done. It's worth bearing in mind here that, as already discussed, an eventual resolution may run directly counter to the disputant's original sense of what is fair and just; this is particularly likely in family law cases where money and children are in dispute.

On top of this, litigants are faced with a system that has evolved over decades to be operated and understood by highly trained lawyers, immersed in the law, not individuals being faced with these issues for the first time, and without training – issues that are, to boot, likely to be highly emotional. Given all this, it is no surprise that front-line staff working in courts and the voluntary sector report that a good proportion of self-representing litigants coming before the court today are prone to angry outbursts (Low Commission, 2015: 14). Such frustration is unsurprising. Today's litigant is an outsider to a system that is unready to help and thinks of his dispute as his own business, but at the very same time refuses to admit that the idiosyncrasies of his dispute have any bearing on the case.

What makes this problem particularly grievous is that those who experience civil justice problems are disproportionately likely to belong to socially-disadvantaged groups. Roughly a third of people in England and Wales have experienced a civil justice problem, according to data from the Civil and Social Justice Panel Survey (CSJPS) (Pleasence et al, 2011: ii). These problems are linked to social factors. Those belonging to social groups at particular risk of exclusion – for example, lone parents, people with disabilities, mental health service users – are more likely to report having a civil justice problem, and are more likely to have experienced multiple problems in their life (Pleasence et al, 2011: ii). They are people, in other words, who are particularly likely to have experienced social injustice and distrust social authorities. It is of note that the CSJPS reveals that those who experience multiple civil justice problems are less likely than the general population to believe that the courts provide a fair hearing (Pleasence et al, 2011: 54). The recent reforms to legal aid are likely to have compounded this sense of pessimism around justice and the law.

It is of note here that, as part of the provisions under LASPO, the government axed the Legal Services Research Centre, which may have given valuable insights into this set of issues. This independent research unit was part of the former Legal Services Commission and published the findings of the CSJPS, the central resource used by the Commission to assess the 'need for, and provision of…legal aid services' (Cleary and Huskinson, 2012: 2). The demise of the Centre, and its flagship survey, has left a gap in our knowledge concerning the use and effectiveness of legal aid for those pursuing justice. A gap that is all the more noticeable since the 2012 reforms came into effect, and their impact has begun to bite.

Conclusion

This chapter has sought to set out a new agenda for assessing legal aid reform, one that focuses on the distinctive value of legal advice and the impact of its retrenchment on people seeking justice. These are areas that have received very little attention in policy debate and academic research. Where the impact of LASPO on legal assistance has been considered – by, for example, the Low Commission (2014; 2015) – the focus is on the emergence of advice 'deserts'. These had been exacerbated by the introduction of a set budget for legal aid expenditure. This had first been suggested by the previous administration when considering introducing a hard cap to legal aid spending in a 1995 green paper. This chapter has aimed to address this omission by exploring the role of the solicitor in settling disputes and how this compares with the work done by mediators. The lack of attention to such issues is partly due to a key shift in policy and political discourse whereby disputes have come to be seen as private matters that reflect personal choices and are best resolved by getting people to sit down and reach a mutually-beneficial outcome. As argued in the second half of this chapter, this ignores the role that power and inequality play in creating disputes and negotiating a settlement. In this context, the role of solicitors in facilitating arm's-length negotiation and protecting their clients' interests can play an essential role in ensuring access to justice. It also serves as a means of bridging the gap between a lay understanding of justice and that enshrined in law. This process of accommodation, we suggest, is essential if those settling a dispute – whether that's in a pre-litigant settlement or in the courtroom – are to feel that justice has been done.

5
REFOCUSING THE DEBATE ABOUT LEGAL AID

We started this book by suggesting that recent reforms represent a wholesale shift in the operation and meaning of legal aid in England and Wales. Once seen as a form of social welfare, since the mid-1980s legal aid has come to be framed as a benefit operating extrinsically to the legal system and understood in primarily economic terms. The most striking evidence of this is the focus in policy debates on the cost of legal aid to the taxpayer. This framing has become so dominant as to normalise the idea that England and Wales has an unacceptably expensive scheme. This is anathema to the original conception of legal aid as a provision available to nearly all, according to their need. The more important observation is that debates about the principles and purpose of legal aid have been squeezed out by the almost exclusive focus on spending. By way of conclusion, we suggest that the debate about legal aid should be refocused on four key issues: the social value and function of legal aid, the impact of the cuts on people seeking advice or access to justice, a broader conception of spending, and the diffuse effects of the cuts on justice and the legal system.

The social value of legal aid

Chapter Two pointed out that the recent reforms have been based on a shift in thinking whereby legal aid has come to be framed as a purely personal benefit, based on an autonomous decision to go to court. Recast in this way, the case for reducing coverage and eligibility is easy to make: why should taxpayers fund individuals to pursue their own personal interests in court? This represents the most significant shift in thinking about legal aid in its tumultuous 65-year history, and has provided the intellectual basis for its most comprehensive recomposition.

We believe that the official conception of legal aid is misguided, and for a number of reasons. First, there is an overemphasis on the degree of personal choice involved in pursuing a legal remedy. For the person dealing with the consequences of medical negligence the only route to compensation in our society is a legal one, or at the very least, it involves the threat of such action. For the person about to be illegally evicted by a private landlord, the law generally constitutes the only means of redress. For the person trying to decide child contact arrangements with a completely unresponsive and combative ex-partner, court remains the only option of settling a dispute. For the person wishing to file for divorce, the court is the only means of doing so. Thus, the idea of a true 'choice' is an erroneous one: it is a Hobson's choice[1] between the expense and stress of a legal route, or no redress at all.

Reinstating the idea that legal dispute is a product of social arrangements is absolutely essential if the case for legal aid is to be won. Among other things, it leads to the conclusion that the increase in people using legal aid over the past quarter century is due not to people recklessly using a 'free' scheme, but because more areas of our life and a greater proportion of our relationships are now governed by legally-binding contracts and statutory protections. In other words, the decision to pursue litigation is very often affected by circumstances that are *outside* an individual's control. This helps explain why adjudication has remained just as popular a route to civil justice after the most recent round of reforms. Most people don't go to court because they want to; they go because they feel that they have to.

We want to suggest something further here: as the originator of laws, regulations and official rules, the state has a responsibility to ensure people's access to legal help to understand and if necessary challenge its decisions. This means that if the state seeks to, for example, alter the administration of social welfare benefits or introduce new criminal offences, it must be clear on how it intends to extend legal help to people affected by these changes. This, again, requires a shift in thinking. It means approaching legal aid in terms of the work done by the legislature, and seeing the former as a feature of the legal system, rather than a standalone benefit. In thinking along these lines, we're borrowing an idea from political philosophy – notably Forst (2014) – that citizens have a right not just to *justice*, but to *justification*. That is, an explanation for official actions and decisions that is clear, cogent and above all coherent to the recipient. Put differently, the modern democratic state has a responsibility to bridge the gap between disputants' sense of justice and the legal meaning of justice. As discussed in Chapter Three, legal advice historically served this purpose. The erosion of this service might have received considerably less attention in policy and public debate than the cuts to legal representation, but this book has sought to argue that its role is just as crucial in ensuring access to justice. Indeed, its role is arguably even more crucial in limiting the costs of the justice system, by reducing the number of cases that actually end up at court, and in fostering a belief that justice has been done, by ensuring the parties understand the process and the rationale behind it.

The benefits of legal advice have been largely ignored, to such a degree that the attempt to replace this form of support with mediation has received little critical scrutiny in debates about legal aid. In Chapter Two we charted the shifting conception of legal aid in policy and practice. A key moment in this story was the rise of alternative dispute resolution, and particularly mediation, as a remedy of 'first resort' for civil legal matters. This shift was first apparent in the mid-1990s, but has been significantly hastened by the recent reforms. In Chapter Four we compared mediation to legal advice. Not, as we pointed out there, because mediation is always and inherently more suitable, as the government has attempted to suggest, but to gain a keener sense of what has been lost in legal aid reform. The transformation of mediation into a remedy of 'first resort' reflects, again, an asocial view of dispute, one that takes civil justice problems to be best solved if parties sit down together to discover a mutually-beneficial resolution. Such a view ignores that disputes frequently reflect differences in power. Without legal advice and advocacy, there's a strong possibility that an asymmetrical relationship will give rise to a settlement that further entrenches that inequality.

The impact for unrepresented litigants and people seeking legal advice

Ironically, considering that civil legal dispute has been recast as a private matter, the individual litigant is poorly understood, and given little attention in recent policy and research. This, as we discussed in Chapter Two, is in stark contrast to the 1960s, where a significant cornerstone of the debate was about the extension of the legal advisory service on the basis that there was an 'unmet need' for support. Today, the policy debate about the extent, impact and importance of support and advice has largely gone, replaced by quantitative and financial considerations. What is neglected in all this is the disputant's experience of seeking justice. The limited research that does exist suggests that the Legal Aid, Sentencing and Punishment of Offenders Act 2012 (LASPO) has had an adverse effect on people pursuing justice. We know, for example, that those seeking legal advice are now met with a stark gap in services: recall the observation in the Low Commission's (2015) report that 92% of advisors at Citizens Advice Bureaux report having nowhere to refer people seeking such support. And where litigants are reaching the courtroom, the experience is baffling and frustrating: as discussed in Chapter Three, anecdotal accounts from courtroom staff point to an increase in angry outbursts from litigants in person (LiPs).

There's another problem here, one discussed at length in Chapter Four: the cuts have been undertaken without any thoroughgoing consideration of the broad spectrum of work that lawyers do to move litigants through the settlement process. A striking example of this is the government's failure to persuade people to move to mediation in place of seeking legal advice and assistance to resolve disputes. A recent House of Commons Justice Committee review of LASPO found that, despite expecting mediation cases to rise by 74% and putting in place provision for this increase, the reality was that the number of mediations in England and Wales *fell* in 2013/14 by 38% (House of Commons Justice Committee, 2015: paragraph 1.6). To explain this, the Committee pointed out that lawyers are traditionally responsible for referring people to mediation, and in restricting the public's access to publicly funded legal assistance the government has inadvertently removed this referral service.

We might add here that a similar argument can be made for the failure of the government's telephone gateway service and the Exceptional Cases Scheme. The take-up of both, in many circumstances, depend on advice from a trusted legal professional, or a level of understanding and knowledge about the operation of the system that is likely to be beyond the vast majority of unrepresented parties. To a limited extent, schemes such as CLOCK, discussed in Chapter Three, are attempting to plug this gap, with some useful signposting and support carried out by volunteer students. But this does leave a big question mark over the values behind a justice system underpinned by and relying on the good will of a volunteers, perhaps analogous to the huge lacuna in the welfare system currently being plugged by food banks. In 21st century Britain, it seems a retrograde step that matters as fundamental to good governance as ensuring a country's citizens have access to justice and food can be left to the charitable instincts of individuals, in a way that seems more reminiscent of Victorian than modern times.

Reassessing legal aid expenditure

If a government has not assessed the social benefit of legal aid, or how it shapes litigants' experience of justice and the legal system, then how can it decide how much spending is too much, or what spending is 'successful'? This should be the counterpoint to the government's argument that we spend too much on legal aid in England and Wales. Without this critical perspective asking for value and function to be brought back into focus, we risk knowing the cost of everything, and the value of nothing.

There are other reasons to object to the current view that we spend 'too much' on legal aid. The basis for this argument is that England and Wales spends significantly more per capita than most other European jurisdictions. There are, of course, two possible interpretations of why England and Wales spend more than most other jurisdictions on legal aid. One view sees the higher rate of spending as evidence of excess and costliness, and another prefers to see it as evidence of world-leading provision. The government view – that the higher rate of spending is a bad thing – has rarely been challenged in public debate, or at least, the media retelling of this debate has tended to obscure critical voices. Nor, we might add, has the basis for this calculation of spending been subject to much critical scrutiny in media debates. In Chapter Two we pointed out that spending on direct legal aid is higher in England and Wales than in other jurisdictions, but other jurisdictions spend more on in-court services. As Bowles and Perry (2009) indicate in their comparative study of legal aid, this balance of direct and indirect support for the litigant reflects the composition and orientation of a legal system. We have an adversarial system, making it exceptionally hard for people to navigate the system without direct legal help. It is jargon-heavy, subject to complex rules of communication and evidence, and does not permit courtroom participants beyond the legal advocate to assist the litigant in putting forward an argument. As discussed in Chapter Two, a reorganisation of legal aid therefore needs a systems-approach, one that considers the nature and needs of the legal system as a whole, as well as the balance of direct and indirect legal support. Without this, the likely consequence is unordered and ineffective change – the situation post-LASPO is evidence of this.

Finally, any assessment of legal aid expenditure should consider the wider impact on other areas of social welfare – a point made very effectively by the recent Low Commission (2014; 2015) reports. Put simply: moving the treatment of a problem from one budget (legal aid) to another (housing, social services, health, police) is no saving overall. The current focus on legal aid spending is thus too narrow and misses much of the impact, both positive and negative, caused by factors surrounding the apparent 'black and white' of a court case. These can be as varied as depression, family breakdown, homelessness, alcoholism and social crises leading to interventions by social services or the police. To admit that these are aspects of legal dispute is, again, to admit to their essentially social character.

The impact of the crisis in legal aid on the legal system

We have argued that seeing the cuts to legal aid in terms of discrete and measurable consequences is to miss its role in ensuring access to justice and ameliorating a range of social problems. The wide-ranging effect of the recent reforms goes beyond this. As suggested at various points in this book, the cuts have also affected the operation of the legal system. The most obvious impact here is the 'delawyering' of legal dispute, touched on earlier. Another is the significant increase in LiPs. This has increased pressure on clerks, judges and legal advocates to offer legal assistance to LiPs, and thus reshaped their role. It is of note here that the Law Society, Chartered Institute of Legal Executives, and the Bar Council (2015a, 2015b, 2015c) have seen cause to produce new guidelines for lawyers and LiPs to clarify their responsibilities and rights in the courtroom post-LASPO. The compound effect of these changes in role and procedure is a move away from an adversarial model of justice, and towards a more inquisitorial system where the judge plays a more participatory role. There are two things that strike us as important here. Firstly, that this shift is a forced one that has occurred without planning or safeguards. Secondly, that it's a change to the operation of the legal system that has occurred without any public debate.

There is another crucial way in which the cuts to legal aid affect our legal system, and again without any thoroughgoing debate. Adjudication provides a means of testing our laws and, with that, our dominant values. Legal aid is especially important here, allowing for test cases and particularly tricky hearings to reach our courts and on occasion reformulate the law. The point was made particularly effectively by the head of the Civil Liberties Department and Police Actions Team at a major firm of solicitors in response to Jackson's (2010) review of civil litigation costs. He said, '[l]egal aid work is essential in terms of access to justice, holding public authorities to account and to the bringing of cases that clarify/develop the law' (Jackson, 2010: 67). Take, by way of a recent example, the outgoing Chief Coroner's call for the government to provide legal aid support for relatives pursuing inquests into unlawful deaths of loved ones (Chief Coroner, 2016). Without such support, miscarriages of justice are less likely to be detected, bad practice more likely to persist, and inadequate statutory measures remain in place.

Conclusion

This discussion has pointed out a range of shared social costs to the removal of legal aid, and suggested that these can only be brought to the fore if we recognise the value and function of this social welfare provision. From this, we conclude that 'the crisis of legal aid' in fact runs much deeper than changes to provision: it results in a court system facing collapse, a legal system facing disordered change, and litigants left to steer through the rough waters of legal dispute without the guidance of legal advice and assistance.

The main focus of this book has been the impact for LiPs involved in family disputes. The highly personal and emotional nature of such disputes, where the stakes can include a person's home and children is perhaps one of the most obvious places where a cut in legal funding and a lack of legal support and advice will be most disastrously experienced. However, it should not be forgotten that these reforms also affect a myriad of other issues, such as employment tribunals adjudicating on someone's livelihood; medical negligence cases and personal injury claims, which may have caused people life-changing injuries; and perhaps most topically the ability to access representation for refugees. Thus, these reforms materially affect a person's ability to access justice across some of the most fundamental areas – where the idea of a free-will 'choice' about starting proceedings is questionable, the issues at law are complex, and the ability to navigate these successfully without legal advice and assistance is bordering on impossible.

Note

[1] In theory a free choice, but in fact only one thing is offered: so you can take it or take nothing.

LIST OF STATUTES

Civil Proceedings, Family Proceedings, and Upper Tribunal Fees (Amendment) Order 2016.

Family and Children Act, 2013.

Family Law Act, 1996.

Legal Aid, Sentencing and Punishment of Offenders Act, 2012.

REFERENCES

Ashton, J.C. (2016) *Legal Education: community impact and outreach of the CLOCK legal companion scheme*. Paper at Celebrating Excellence in Law Teaching Conference, University of Oxford, July 2016.

Bawdon, F. and Hynes, S. (2011) *London Advice Watch: Findings of a research project on provision of social welfare law advice in London*. Trust for London and Legal Action Group. Available at http://www.lag.org.uk/media/47814/london_advice_watch_report.pdf.

BBC (2014) 'Lawyers stage second walkout over legal aid cuts'. 7 March 2014. Available at http://www.bbc.co.uk/news/uk-26472809.

BBC News (1998) 'Legal services shake-up announced'. 2 December 1998. Available at http://news.bbc.co.uk/1/hi/uk_politics/226653.stm.

Boulle, L. and Nesic, M. (2001) *Mediation: Principles, Process, Procedure*. London: Butterworths.

Bowcott, O. (2014) 'Appeal court judge 'horrified' at number of litigants without lawyers', *The Guardian*. 23 November 2014. Available at https://www.theguardian.com/law/2014/nov/23/appeal-court-judge-horrified-number-litigants-without-lawyers.

Bowles, R. and Perry, A. (2009) *International comparison of publicly funded legal services and justice systems*, Ministry of Justice research series 14/09, October 2009.

Cape, E. and Moorhead, R. (2005) *Demand Induced Supply? Identifying Cost Drivers in Criminal Defence Work – A report to the Legal Services Commission*. London: Legal Services Commission Research Centre.

Cappeletti, M and Garth, B. (1981) 'Introduction: Access to Justice and the Welfare State', in M. Cappelletti and B. Garth (eds) *Access to Justice and the Welfare State*, Alphen aan den Rijn, Netherlands: Sijthoff and Noordhoff.

Carter, P. (2006) 'Lord Carter's Reform of Legal Aid Procurement. Legal Aid: A market-based approach to reform'. London: Department of Constitutional Affairs.

Chief Coroner (2016) 'Report of the Chief Coroner to the Lord Chancellor: Third Annual Report 2015-16'. London: H.M.S.O.

Cleary, A. and Huskinson, T. (2012) *The English and Welsh Civil and Social Justice Survey Panel Survey: Wave Two Technical Report*. Legal Services Commission and Ipsos Mori. Available at http://webarchive. nationalarchives.gov.uk/20130315183909/http://www.justice. gov.uk/downloads/publications/research-and-analysis/lsrc/csjps-wave2.pdf.

CLOCK (2016) Community Legal Outreach Collaboration Keele. Available at https://www.keele.ac.uk/law/ legaloutreachcollaboration/.

Committee on Economic, Social and Cultural Rights (2016) 'Concluding Observations of the Sixth Periodic Report on the United Kingdom of Great Britain and Northern Ireland'. Available at http://tbinternet.ohchr.org/_layouts/treatybodyexternal/ SessionDetails1.aspx?SessionID=1059&Lang=en.

Committee on the Elimination of Discrimination against Women (2013) 'Concluding Observations of the Seventh Periodic Report on the United kingdom of Great Britain and Northern Ireland'. Available at http://www.edf.org.uk/blog/ehrc-submission-to-the-un-committee-on-the-elimination-of-all-forms-of-discrimination-against-women/.

Cookson, G. (2011) *Unintended Consequences: The Cost of the Government's Legal Aid Reforms*. London: King's College London.

Cookson, G. (2013) 'Analysing the Economic Justification for the Reforms to Social Welfare and Family Law Legal Aid', *Journal of Social Welfare and Family Law,* 35(1): 21-41.

REFERENCES

Dannemann, G (1996) 'Access to Justice: An Anglo-German Comparison', *European Public Law*, 2 (2): 271-92.

Davis, G., Cretney, S. and Collins, J.G. (1994) *Simple Quarrels*. Oxford: Oxford University Press.

Department of Constitutional Affairs (2005) *A Fairer Deal for Legal Aid*. Available at https://www.gov.uk/government/uploads/system/uploads/attachment_data/file/272138/6591.pdf.

Dingwall, R. and Eekelaar, J. (1988) *Divorce Mediation and the Legal Process*. Oxford: Clarendon Press.

Eekelaar, J. and Maclean, M (2013) *Family Justice: The Work of Family Judges in Uncertain Times*. Oxford: Hart Publishing.

Eekelaar, J., Maclean, M. and Beinart, S. (2000) *Family Lawyers: The Divorce Work of Solicitors*. Oxford: Hart Publishing.

European Commission for the Efficiency of Justice (2016) *European Judicial Systems: Efficiency and quality of justice*. Council of Europe. Available at http://www.coe.int/t/dghl/cooperation/cepej/evaluation/2016/publication/REV1/2016_1%20-%20CEPEJ%20Study%2023%20-%20General%20report%20-%20EN.pdf.

Family Mediation Council (2016) 'Code of Practice for Family Mediators, September 2016'. Available at http://www.familymediationcouncil.org.uk/wp-content/uploads/2016/09/FMC-Code-of-Practice-September-2016-2.pdf.

Forst R. (2014) *The Right to Justification: Elements of a Constructivist Theory of Justice*. New York: Columbia University Press.

Garth B.G and Capelletti M. (1978) 'Access to Justice: The newest wave in the worldwide movement to make rights effective', *Articles by Maurer Faculty*, Paper, No. 1142. Available at http://www.repository.law.indiana.edu/facpub/1142.

Garth B.G. (1980) *Neighbourhood Law Firms for the Poor: A comparative study of recent development in legal aid and in the legal profession*. London: Springer.

Genn, H. (2010) *Judging Civil Justice*. Cambridge: Cambridge University Press.

Genn, H. and Beinart, S. (1999) *Paths to Justice: What People Do and Think About Going to Law*. London: Hart Publishing.

Goriely, T. and Paterson, A. (1996) 'Introduction', in A. Paterson and T. Goriely (eds) *A Reader on Resourcing Civil Justice*, Oxford: Oxford University Press, pp 1–24.

Gove, M. (2016) 'Changes to criminal legal aid contracting: Written statement to Parliament'. Available at https://www.gov.uk/government/speeches/changes-to-criminal-legal-aid-contracting.

Grimwood, G.G. (2015) 'Controversy in 2010/11 surrounding the Government's plans for legal aid reform', House of Commons Briefing Paper, No. 05850.

Hitchings, E. and Miles, J. (2016) 'Mediation, financial remedies, information provision and legal advice: the post-LASPO conundrum', *Journal of Social Welfare and Family Law*, 38(2): 175-95.

Hitchings, E., Miles, J. and Woodward, H. (2013) *Assembling the Jigsaw Puzzle: Understanding financial settlement on divorce*. University of Bristol research report. Available at http://www.bristol.ac.uk/media-library/sites/law/migrated/documents/assemblingthejigsawpuzzle.pdf.

House of Commons Justice Committee (2011) 'Government's Proposed Reform of Legal Aid: Third Report of Session 2010-11, Vol. 1', London: HMSO.

House of Commons Justice Committee (2015) *8th Report, Impact of Changes to Civil Legal Aid under Part 1 of the Legal Aid, Sentencing and Punishment of Offenders Act 2012*. London: House of Commons. Available at http://www.publications.parliament.uk/pa/cm201415/cmselect/cmjust/311/31103.htm.

House of Lords Debate (HL Deb) (2011), 19 May, 727, cols 1535-62.

Hyde, J. (2015) 'Rise of LiPs not causing delays, says courts chief', *The Law Society Gazette*. 14 October 2015. Available at http://www.lawgazette.co.uk/law/rise-of-lips-not-causing-delays-says-courts-chief/5051567.fullarticle.

Hynes, S. (2012) *Austerity Justice*. London: Legal Action Group.

Hynes, S. (2014) 'Lies, Damned Lies, and Legal Aid Statistics', News comment for Legal Action Group, November 2014. Available at http://www.lag.org.uk/magazine/2014/11/news-comment-lies,-damn-lies-and-legal-aid-statistics.aspx.

REFERENCES

Hynes, S. and Robins, J. (2009) *The Justice Gap: Whatever Happened to Legal Aid?* London: Legal Action Group.

Ingleby, R. (1992) *Solicitors and Divorce.* Oxford: Oxford University Press.

Jackson R. (2010) *Review of Civil Litigation Costs – Final Report.* London: The Stationery Office. Available at https://www.judiciary.gov.uk/wp-content/uploads/JCO/Documents/Reports/jackson-final-report-140110.pdf.

Judicial Office (2016) *Reforming the courts' approach to McKenzie Friends – A Consultation.* Available at https://www.judiciary.gov.uk/wp-content/uploads/2016/02/mf-consultation-paper-feb2016-1.pdf.

Kempson E. (1989) *Legal Advice and Assistance.* London: Policy Studies Institute.

Knight, B (2014) *Innovation in Law Report 2014.* Available at https://www.hja.net/wp-content/uploads/hja-innovation-in-law-report-2014.pdf.

Law Centres Network (2016) 'List of Law Centres'. http://www.lawcentres.org.uk/about-law-centres/law-centres-on-google-maps/alphabetically.

Law Council of Australia (2016) 'Budget does nothing to address crisis in legal aid', Media release, No. 1621. Available at https://www.lawcouncil.asn.au/lawcouncil/images/1621_--_Budget_does_nothing_to_lift_legal_aid_out_of_crisis.pdf.

The Law Society, Chartered Institute of Legal Executives, and the Bar Council (2015a) 'Litigants in person: guidelines for lawyers'. Available at http://www.barcouncil.org.uk/media/351220/litigants_in_person_guidelines_for_lawyers_-_1_june_2015.pdf.

The Law Society, Chartered Institute of Legal Executives, and the Bar Council (2015b) 'Litigants in person: notes for clients'. Available at http://www.barcouncil.org.uk/media/351223/litigants_in_person_guidelines_for_lawyers_notes_for_clients.pdf.

The Law Society, Chartered Institute of Legal Executives, and the Bar Council (2015c) 'Litigants in person: notes for litigants in person'. Available at http://www.barcouncil.org.uk/media/351226/litigants_in_person_guidelines_for_lawyers_notes_for_lips.pdf.

Law Society Gazette (2016) 'Contact centre forced to close by legal aid cuts'. 11 July 2016. Available at http://www.lawgazette.co.uk/law/contact-centre-forced-to-close-by-legal-aid-cuts/5056436.article.

Leat, D. (1975) 'The Rise and Role of the Poor Man's Lawyer', *British Journal of Law and Society*, 2(2): 166-81.

LECG (2006) *Legal Aid Reforms Proposed by the Carter Review – Analysis and Commentary*. London: LECG Ltd. Available at https://www.lccsa.org.uk/assets/documents/consultation/carter%20analysis.pdf.

Legal Action Group (2010) *Social welfare law: What the public wants from civil legal aid – Findings from a nationwide opinion poll*. Available at http://www.lag.org.uk/media/47770/social_welfare_law_what_the_public_wants_from_civil_legal_aid.pdf.

Legal Action Group (2014) *Legal aid at 65: Is the government losing the argument over cuts?* Available at http://www.lag.org.uk/media/175004/legal_aid_at_65.pdf.

Legal Aid Board (1995) *Legal Aid – Targeting Need: The Future of Publicly Funded Help in Solving Legal Problems and Disputes in England and Wales*. London: Legal Aid Board.

Lewis, P.S.C. (2000) *Assumptions about Lawyers in Policy Statements: A Survey of Relevant Research*. Lord Chancellor's Department Research Programme.

Liebmann, M. (2011) 'History and Overview of Mediation in the UK', in M. Liebmann (ed.) *Mediation in Context*, London: Jessica Kingsley.

Lithman, N. QC (2014) 'CBA Chairman's Update: Nigel Lithman QC'. Available at https://www.criminalbar.com/latest-updates/news/q/date/2014/03/10/monday-message-10-03-14/.

Lord Chancellor's Office (1995) *Legal Aid: Targeting Need*. London: Her Majesty's Stationery Office (HMSO).

Lord Chancellor's Office (1998) *Modernising Justice: The Government's Plans for Reforming Legal Services and Courts*. London: HMSO.

The Low Commission (2014) *Tackling the Advice Deficit: A strategy for access to advice and legal support on social welfare law in England and Wales*. Available at http://www.lowcommission.org.uk/dyn/1389221772932/Low-Commission-Report-FINAL-VERSION.pdf.

The Low Commission (2015) *Getting it Right in Social Welfare Law: The Low Commission's follow-up report*. Available at http://www. lowcommission.org.uk/dyn/1435772523695/Getting_it_Right_ Report_web.pdf.

Luban, D. (1988) *Lawyers and Justice: An Ethical Study*. Princeton, NJ: Princeton University Press.

Maclean, M. and Eekelaar, J. (2009) *Family Law Advocacy: How Barristers help the Victims of Family Failure*. Oxford: Hart Publishing.

Maclean, M. and Eekelaar, J. (2016) *Lawyers and Mediators: The Brave New World of Services for Separating Families*. Oxford: Hart Publishing.

Magistrates Association (2015) 'Survey on litigants in person and unrepresented defendants'. Available at https://www. magistrates-association.org.uk/sites/magistrates-association.org.uk/ files/01%20Survey%20on%20litigants%20in%20person%20and%20 unrepresented%20defendants%2013%20January%202015.pdf.

Magistrates Association (2016) 'Response to reforming the courts' approach to McKenzie Friends: Consultation by the Judicial Office'. Available at https://www.magistrates-association.org.uk/ sites/magistrates-association.org.uk/files/10%20McKenzie%20 Friends%20consultation%20response%2008%2006%2016.pdf.

Manchester, A.H. and Whetton, J.M. (1974) 'Marital Conciliation in England and Wales', *International and Comparative Law Quarterly*, 23(2): 339.

Manson, J. (2012) *Public Services on the Brink*. Exeter, UK: Imprint Academic.

McGuinness, T. (2016) *Changes to Criminal Legal Aid*, House of Commons Briefing Paper, No. 6628.

Ministry of Justice (2010) 'Proposals for the Reform of Legal Aid in England and Wales'. Available at https://www.gov.uk/government/ uploads/system/uploads/attachment_data/file/228970/7967.pdf.

Ministry of Justice (2011a) 'Reform of Legal Aid in England and Wales: the Government Response'. Available at https://www. gov.uk/government/uploads/system/uploads/attachment_data/ file/228890/8072.pdf.

Ministry of Justice (2016a) 'Family Court Statistics Quarterly, England and Wales: January to March 2016'. Available at https://www.gov.uk/government/uploads/system/uploads/attachment_data/file/533607/family-court-statistics-jan-mar-2016.pdf.

Ministry of Justice (2016b) 'Represent yourself in court'. Available at https://www.gov.uk/represent-yourself-in-court/divorce-and-separation-involving-children.

Ministry of Justice and Legal Aid Agency (2014), 'Legal Aid Statistics, England and Wales, April 2014 to June 2014'. Available at https://www.gov.uk/government/statistics/legal-aid-statistics-april-2014-to-june-2014.

Ministry of Justice and Legal Aid Agency (2016a), 'Legal Aid Statistics, England and Wales, January 2016 to March 2016'. Available at https://www.gov.uk/government/uploads/system/uploads/attachment_data/file/533178/legal-aid-statistics-england-and-wales-bulletin-jan-to-mar_16.pdf.

Ministry of Justice and Legal Aid Agency (2016b) 'User Guide to Legal Aid Statistics, England and Wales'. Available at https://www.gov.uk/government/uploads/system/uploads/attachment_data/file/533336/user-guide-to-legal-aid-statistic-in-england-and-wales.pdf.

Ministry of Justice, Department for Education and the Welsh Government (2011) 'Family Justice Review'. Available at https://www.gov.uk/government/uploads/system/uploads/attachment_data/file/217343/family-justice-review-final-report.pdf.

Myers, R. (2016) 'Don't try to defend yourself in court. But if you have to, here are some crucial tips', *The Guardian*, 26 April 2016. Online edition.

National Audit Office (2014) *Implementing Reforms to Civil Legal Aid,* Report by the Comptroller and Auditor General, National Audit Office, November 2014. Available at http://www.nao.org.uk.

Nottingham Trent University (2016) *Legal Advice Centre*. Available at https://www4.ntu.ac.uk/legal_advice_centre/.

Orchard, S. (2003) 'Evidence Submitted by Stephen Orchard, former Chief Executive, Legal Services Commission', Select Committee on Constitutional Affairs. Available at http://www.publications. parliament.uk/pa/cm200203/cmselect/cmconst/1106/1106we03. htm.

Parkinson, L. (2014) *Family Mediation*. London: Jordan Publishing.

Paterson, A. (2011) *Lawyers and the Public Good*. Cambridge: Cambridge University Press.

Personal Support Unit (2012) 'Personal Support Unit'. Available at https://www.thepsu.org/.

Peysner, J. (2014) *Access to Justice: A Critical Analysis of Recoverable Conditional Fees and No-Win No-Fee Funding*. Basingstoke: Palgrave Macmillan.

Pleasence, Balmer, and Moorhead, (2012) *A Time of Change: Solicitors' Firms in England and Wales.* The Law Society, Legal Services Board, and Ministry of Justice.

Pollock, S. (1975) *Legal Aid: The first 25 years*. London: Oyez Publishing.

Public Accounts Committee (2015) *Thirty Sixth Report: Implementing Reforms to Civil Legal Aid*. Available at http://www.publications. parliament.uk/pa/cm201415/cmselect/cmpubacc/808/80802.htm.

Reed, L. (2014) *The Family Court without a Lawyer: A Handbook for Litigants in Person*. Bath: Bath Publishing.

Reiner, R. (2007) *Law and Order: An Honest Citizen's Guide to Crime and Control*. London: Polity.

Rights of Women, Women's Aid Federation of England, and Welsh Women's Aid (2014) 'Evidencing Domestic Violence: Reviewing the Amended Regulations'. Available at http://rightsofwomen. org.uk/wp-content/uploads/2014/12/Evidencing-domestic-violence-IV.pdf.

Roberts, M. (2005) 'Family mediation: The development of the regulatory framework in the UK', *Conflict Resolution Quarterly,* 22(4): 509.

Roberts, M. (2007) *Developing the Craft of Mediation: Reflections on Theory and Practice*. London: Jessica Kingsley.

Roberts, M. (2014) *Mediation in Family Disputes: Principles and Practice*. 4th edition. Farnham: Ashgate.

Roshier, B. and Teff, H. (2013) *Law and Society in England*. London: Routledge.

Rushcliffe Committee (1945) *Report of the Committee on Legal Aid*. London: HMSO.

Secondary Legislation Scrutiny Committee, HL (2015) 'Draft Civil Proceedings, Family Proceedings, and Upper Tribunal Fees (Amendment) Order 2016'. Available at http://www.publications. parliament.uk/pa/ld201516/ldselect/ldsecleg/78/7802.htm.

Straw J. (2009) 'Constitutional Continuity: LSE Law Department 'Officers of the Law' Lecture Series'. 3 March 2009. Text available at http://www.lse.ac.uk/publicEvents/pdf/20090303_JackStraw.pdf.

Trinder, L., Hunter, R., Hitchings, E. et al. (2014) *Litigants in Person in Private Family Law Cases*. Ministry of Justice Analytical Series. Available at https://www.gov.uk/government/publications/ litigants-in-person-in-private-family-law-cases.

University of Manchester (2016) *School of Law Legal Advice Centre*. Available at http://www.law.manchester.ac.uk/study/discover/ professional-development/legal-advice-centre/.

Ward, R. and Akhtar, A. (2011) *Walker and Walker's English Legal System*. Oxford: Oxford University Press.

Woolf, Lord (1996) *Access to Justice: Final Report*. Department of Constitutional Affairs. Available at http://webarchive. nationalarchives.gov.uk/+/http://www.dca.gov.uk/civil/final/ index.htm.

Zander, M. (2000) *The State of Justice*. London: Sweet and Maxwell.

Index